To darling Mummy
with many good wishes
& lots of love from us all

Maurice, Leila, Nicholas
Susan & Caroline
July 73

OBJECTS OF VERTU

OBJECTS OF VERTU

Howard
Ricketts

 Barrie and Jenkins

First published 1971 by Barrie & Jenkins Ltd.,
2 Clement's Inn, London W.C.2.

Photographs by Michael Plomer
© Barrie & Jenkins Ltd

Text set by Yendall & Company Limited, London.
Colour origination by Colour Workshop Limited, Hertford.
Printed and bound in the Netherlands by
Drukkerij de Lange/van Leer & Co. N.V. Deventer.

ISBN 0 257 65091 1

Contents

Preface

Objects of Vertu may prove to be a mystifying title to the layman. It is a term well-known to collectors of snuff-boxes and related objects of luxury dating from the 18th and 19th centuries. Yet if such a collector should be asked to define this title concisely he might be slightly at a loss to do so. The reason for this is that the word 'vertu' has changed its meaning since the late 17th century. In 1662 a 'man of vertu' was someone 'who had a special interest in or taste for the fine arts . . . a connoisseur who frequently carried on such pursuits in a dilettante or trifling manner'. It wasn't until a century later that Horace Walpole described 'my books, my vertu, and my other follies and amusements'. This narrowed the field (which in earlier days had included geological and natural historical specimens) to small objects of luxury. During the latter part of the 19th century these were to be collected in their own right and were frequently described in sale catalogues as *bibelots* or *objets de vitrine*.

Within the scope of this subject however, which covers a multitude of diverse objects, there are several sub-divisions: for example, snuff-boxes, seals, chatelaines, scent bottles and cane handles. By 1830 snuff-taking was in decline and consequently there was less demand for elaborate portable boxes and associated objects. They were out of keeping with the more severe style of dress which came in in the early Victorian period, and from then until Carl Fabergé revived objects of vertu – first seen outside Russia at the Paris Universal Exhibition in 1900 – the goldsmith and enameller's art concentrated on ornamental objects for the house. It was at this time that art collecting became fashionable; Renaissance gold-mounted hardstone cups together with Limoges painted enamels were keenly sought after and expensive and as a result both copies and imitations made to deceive emerged from the workshops of Europe.

The art of the enameller is taken as a guide-line throughout this book, which is an attempt to project the individual objects as well as the work of key craftsmen into a social context. Such a survey, in the space allowed, can only afford to be superficial, and a select bibliography has been provided at the back of this book for those readers who have a more specialist interest.

Acknowledgements

I should like to thank Mr Kenneth Snowman who has given me valuable help and has also allowed me to photograph objects of vertu from the collection of Messrs. Wartski. Doctor Wilhelm Mrazek, Director of the Österreichisches Museum für angewandte Kunst, Vienna, redirected my researches in Viennese enamels.

I should also like to express my gratitude to Mr M. Hakim and Mr David Lavender who have allowed me to select pieces for photography.

Mr John Hayward, Mr Ian Venture, Mr Philip Coole, Mr Paul Basil, Miss Caroline Ferard and Mr Robert Woolley have also given me assistance. But above all I would like to acknowledge the help and assistance given me by my wife in the fields of translation, research and in the typing of the manuscript.

I am greatly indebted to the following private collectors, museums and antique dealers who have kindly allowed me to take photographs of objects of vertu in their possession: Mrs Viva King, Messrs. Park Antiques, the Victoria and Albert Museum, Sotheby & Co., Parke-Bernet Galleries Inc, Messrs. Wartski Ltd.

I am also grateful to those authors who have given permission to quote passages which appear in the text.

Introduction

The first true objects of vertu emerged during the late Renaissance period in Western Europe. In the Middle Ages patronage lay mainly in the hands of the church and it wasn't until the Renaissance that this 'mediaeval instinct that subjugated individual pride to corporate loyalty was dead'.[1] The 16th century was to be the age of individualism in Italy which was to have a marked effect on Gothic Northern Europe. The artist himself was allowed more freedom but his work had to glorify the individualism of his patron. Europe was rich; in the course of the 16th century the amount of money in circulation was quadrupled and Italy became the richest country. The Princes governed by 'sheer weight of power'.[2] In artistic circles the theory of 'continuous upward progress was fortified by the belief that a similar development had taken place in Greece'.[3] It was the classical period that provided inspiration.

Some of the great goldsmiths were also sculptors or painters. There was less of a division between the crafts than exists today. Artists and craftsmen travelled from court to court; unlike during the previous centuries they were known by name and their success depended on their reputation. The lapidaries of Italy made splendid objects for the reigning houses of Europe; mounted hardstone pieces can be found in the great treasuries of Europe in large numbers.[4] The hardstone tazza illustrated is elaborately mounted in gold; it is interesting to compare this with a supremely simple Roman agate scent bottle modestly mounted during the 16th century so as not to detract from the markings of the stone. The art of the goldsmith emerges in many household objects during this period – a knife and fork contained in a tooled leather travelling case are chased with figures and then enriched with enamel. In this example, as in Renaissance jewellery, the ground is cut with irregular grooves to give a base to the enamel. These were probably made in Antwerp which, during the 16th century, c. 1570, was one of the most flourishing ports in Europe and the principal port of the Low Countries. This attracted craftsmen who found a good market for luxury objects amongst the rich merchants as well as for the export trade.

In Germany the two most prominent centres were Augsburg and Nuremberg. Both had a flourishing trade with Lisbon, Venice, Antwerp and, eventually, the Americas and together with Munich and Prague were the true home of the Renaissance.[5] It was from Augsburg that most of the more elaborate enamelled objects came during the latter part of the 17th century. Toilet sets in silver, some elaborately enclosed in architectural cases, are enriched with painted enamel panels. Painted enamels had been common in Northern Italy and in France since the early 16th century. The town of Limoges had produced a seemingly unending supply of objects

[1] Evans, J., *Pattern* (see Bibliography), p. 14.

[2] ibid., p. 14.

[3] Pope-Hennessy, John, *Italian High Renaissance and Baroque Sculpture*, Phaidon Press, London, 1963.

[4] In the Schatzkammer der Residenz, Munich, and also in the Treasury at Vienna.

[5] *Larousse Encyclopedia of Renaissance and Baroque Art*, general ed. René Huyghe, Hamlyn, London, 1966, p. 175.

both secular and liturgical, but the painted enamels of Augsburg, mainly executed at the end of the 17th century and the beginning of the 18th, display a degree of quality seen only in contemporary watch cases, particularly those by the Huaud family.

The workshops of England, Holland and Germany were swelled by an influx of Huguenot craftsmen after they no longer enjoyed religious freedom when the Edict of Nantes was revoked in 1685. These refugees stimulated the existing centres of goldsmiths, and in some cases provided skills which were hitherto unknown and which were to form the basis of a national craft.

The 17th century had seen devastating warfare and economic problems facing many countries in Europe; it proved to be the beginning of the decline of Hapsburg power in Europe, and in France all power was transferred from the Church to the State. The construction of Versailles was commenced and the national workshops of France, started in the 16th century, kept active.

An Italian jasper tazza.
From the circle of artists working at the court of Cosimo I, Grand Duke of Tuscany; second half of the 16th century.
6½ in. high.
Parke-Bernet Galleries Inc., New York

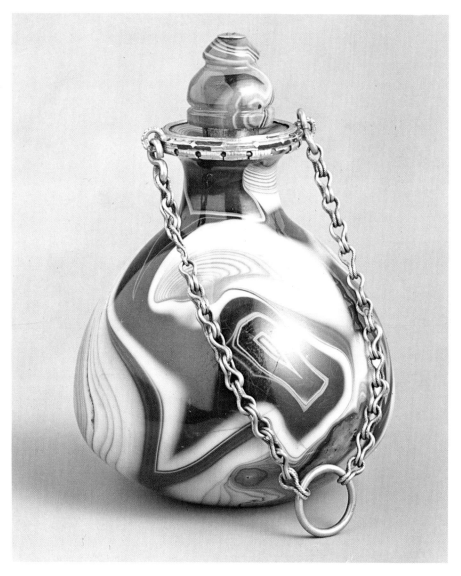

Already the fashion for snuffing had taken hold in some parts of Europe; yet because the Roi Soleil disapproved of it snuff-taking had few adherents at Versailles. The extraordinary popularity of this habit during the following century was to allow for the manufacture of snuff-boxes and other related objects of vertu, which, as decorative and extravagant luxuries, rivalled the opulence reflected in Renaissance goldsmiths' work. Had Louis XIV not shown his disapproval, fine 17th century snuff-boxes might well have survived in some quantity until today.

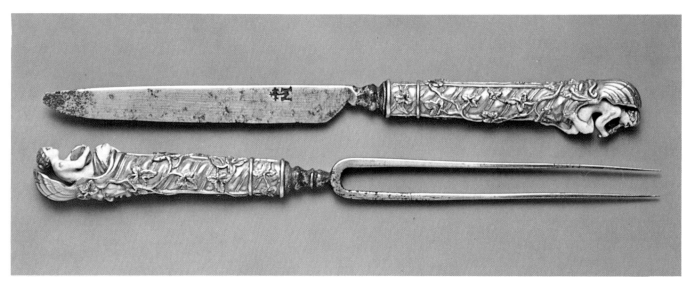

French Snuff Boxes of the 18th Century

The first quarter of the 18th century proved to be a transitional period in the evolution of objects of vertu in Europe. In Saxony Johann Melchior Dinglinger was making fantasy objects for the Elector,[1] whilst the gold-smiths of Paris were beginning to decorate the snuff-box – hitherto a fairly plain receptacle – with the imagination and brilliance that had been lavished on *Schatzkammer* objects during the two previous centuries. They were to lead Europe both in the role of designer and craftsman.

The 17th century in France had been the age of Molière, Le Pautre, Racine and Madame de Sévigné. The gardens at Versailles had been laid out in the grand manner in 1688, but from that time until 1715 – the year of Louis XIV's death – France had been involved in continuous war. It had left Western Europe bankrupt in many areas and France disillusioned with the *Grand Siècle*. But this had not been a sudden development. Since Louis XIV 'had passed beyond his prime of maturity and conquest, the splendours of court were dimmed, and men turned from power to delight. In every department of intellectual and artistic activity there was demand for a quicker measure and a smaller scale. Locke and Hobbes inspired a new generation of politicians and the vast state rooms were cut up into *petits appartements*'.[2] Simon said at Louis XIV's death, '*le peuple, ruiné, accablé, désespéré, redit grâces à Dieu, avec un éclat scandaleux, d'une délivrance dont ses plus ardents désirs ne doutaient pas*'. But now, under a very youthful king ruling through a Regent, society was highly permissive and this was reflected in the ornamentation of works of art. Montesquieu[3] wrote '*ce sont ces différents plaisirs de notre âme qui forment les objets du goût, comme le beau, le bon, l'agréable, le naïf, le délicat, le tendre, le gracieux, le je ne sais quoi*' (sic). This new relaxed attitude created a link between the artist and his public; the artist was received into society, and society itself took to art. The touch of the *amateur* appears in literature, decoration and the fine arts. Fashion in costume as well as for extravagant accessories or objects of vertu took on a new importance.

The *Salon* opened in 1737 and this initiated a gradual corrosion of the monarch's monopoly over artistic talent, and marked the transference of patronage from the king to the educated society of Paris. For the first time the tastes of the 'ordinary man' were felt. Woman had emerged in a more emancipated form; noble ladies without being *femmes savantes*, ruled over the arts and sciences. Women, indeed, set the keynote of Parisian society. It was their choice of ornament which prevailed.

Consequently, the social climate improved during the first half of the 18th century; patronage was in the hands of many and not just in the hands of the monarch; there were moments when the economy was bad, but although the national economic situation deteriorated towards 1790 there was a considerable amount of money in the hands of a broad stratum of society.

[1] von Wartzdorf, E., *Johann Melchior Dinglinger*, Gebr. Mann Verlag, Berlin, 1962.

[2] Evans, op. cit., p. 82.

[3] Montesquieu in his article 'on taste' in Diderot's *L'Encyclopédie*.

A circular snuff-box, the lid enamelled with a miniature of 'La Finette' by Watteau. The enamel almost certainly by Jean-Baptiste Massé, who owned the Watteau at the time, the box by Louis Mailly.
Paris, 1722–6.
2½ in. diameter.

Private collection

Ever since tobacco was brought back from America in the early 16th century it had been either smoked or ground or inhaled as snuff. However it wasn't until early in the following century that tobacco was imported in large quantities into England and Spain – and by 1618 Virginia was yielding over 20,000 lb a year. The habit of snuff-taking became more internationally prevalent in the second half of the century. The Church deeply disapproved of it and attempted to suppress it, associating it with witchcraft. Pope Urban VIII, irritated by those who continued the habit during mass, was moved to issue a Papal Bull threatening excommunication to all offenders. In 1709 in England *The Tatler* spoke out vehemently against the growing fashion of women taking snuff in church; a few years beforehand the habit had become general with the vast quantities of it thrown on to the London market after the capture of Spanish ships loaded with snuff in the action of Vigo Bay.[4] In France Louis XIV showed his disapproval on many occasions and would not permit it in his presence. Consequently 17th century snuff-boxes in gold or precious metal are very rare.

In 1715, with Louis XIV's death, official disapproval was lifted. For the next eight years the young Louis XV ruled under a Regent, and during this permissive period snuff-taking was allowed at Court. The goldsmiths of Paris started to lavish care and attention on the boxes made in the 1720s, but comparatively few of these exist today, although the Regent is known to have had a collection of over several hundred.

French boxes at this date were the most splendid of all in Europe and they were used by the Crown for diplomatic presentations. Two such boxes were made by Daniel Govers, the Royal boxmaker.

[4] Vigo Bay, Action of, see Trevelyan, G. M., *Illustrated English Social History*, Pelican Books, London, 1966, vol. III, p. 48.

Two Louis XV diplomatic presentation snuff-boxes, the first by Jacques-Michel Lemaire and decorated in *piqué* hairwork, Paris 1729. The lower box, by Daniel Govers, the Royal boxmaker, was made in 1726, but presented to Isaac de Thellusson, a Swiss banker, in 1744. Recipients of such diplomatic presentation boxes quite commonly sold them back to the French Foreign Ministry if they so wished. Both 3¼ in. wide.

Sotheby & Co.

It was at this period that the snuff-box took on a new significance. It was said that the standing of a man who was seen to be taking snuff could be gauged by the manner in which he performed the action.[5] The box in the first place counted more than the snuff it contained. The owner required a neat beautiful object to be held in the hand, or taken out of the pocket in order to be offered to other persons, if not necessarily to friends. He would have already selected one of the many different blends of snuff from his merchant – 'A fine old rappee of San Domingo, just arrived', the tobacconist's advertisement might have run. Sacheverell Sitwell in *The Geography of Snuff* goes on to describe the different types available. 'The earlier sorts . . . were Bergamota, Jessamina, Orangery and Neroly, named from the scents from which they were compounded and dating, it is evident, from late in the 17th century. There had been, among the foreign snuffs sold in London, Carotte; Palillio, which was Portuguese in origin; Etienne, offered every year to Louis XV upon his birthday by the different snuff manufacturers of Paris, from which the best was chosen and called by the number of that year'.[6]

[5] Snowman, A. K., *Eighteenth Century Gold Boxes of Europe*, Faber & Faber, London, 1966.

[6] Sitwell, Sacheverell, *Sacred and Profane Love*, Faber & Faber, London, 1940, p. 240.

[7] le Corbeille, Clare, *European and American Snuff-boxes*, Batsford, London, 1966.
[8] The author of *Whipping Tom* (1722), exaggerates the action, 'some betwixt Finger and Thumb hold it perhaps a Quarter of an Hour, not snuffing it, but daubing it . . . under their Nostrils'.

With his snuff-box primed, the beau would then act out the ritual which was to be satirised in periodicals and pamphlets during the 18th century. Taking the box in the left hand he would pass it to his right, tap the box on the lid, open it, present it to those around him and having retrieved it, making sure that it was kept open, he would level the uneven quantity of snuff by tapping it on the side.[7] He would then take a clean pinch of snuff with his right fingers, holding it for several moments,[8] then close his snuff-box.

This was not the end of it. A really fashionable gentleman would own a collection of boxes – for the less enthusiastic a group of four boxes, one for each season, was socially acceptable; for winter a heavy box, and a light one for summer. It was said that a man was exempted from having a library and a natural history room – the ultimate in intellectual status – if he had three-hundred snuff-boxes and as many rings. Few boxes made before 1740 have survived, but after this date production was more prolific. The earlier ones, especially the Royal presentation boxes, were inevitably made to accommodate a portrait miniature inside the lid. The first boxes were decorated still in the manner of Jean Berain with a symmetric design. The bodies of the boxes were severely plain and of attractive cartouche shape.

In the 1730s the effect of the rococo movement was reflected in the design of boxes. The first examples were designed by Juste-Aurèle Meissonnier (1693–1750), displaying rocaille asymmetry: nothing that could be gracefully curved was left straight. Although many larger domestic objects such as ormolu candelabra survive from this period, it is sad that so few truly rococo boxes remain.

Repoussé is the word used to describe the technique of decoration of metal where the surface is worked from the back to achieve the desired raised effect – it is 'pushed forward': the gold plate (in the case of a snuff-box) is then, when this initial stage has been completed, reversed and 'finished' from the front; the chaser might then remodel the repoussé

form and perhaps he might 'granulate' the background with a matting tool to give it a matt effect and so set off the raised figures in the foreground.

    Although this was a popular and fashionable technique in France during the 1730s, it was used in England with more success in the following decade when some of the finest repoussé boxes ever to have been made appeared. The subject matter was generally a mythological theme, and the extravagance of the relief-decoration is often embellished with highly sculptural corner or rim motifs.

An Italian shop scene with snuff-boxes and chatelaines in a case on the counter and jewellery, powder-boxes and sword hilts in the background.
Detail from a picture in the manner of Longhi, second quarter of the 18th century.
Sotheby & Co.

[9] *Tobacco, and its Associations with Bristol*, W. D. & H. O. Wills, Bristol, 1926, p. 16.

A George II *repoussé* cartouche-shaped gold snuff-box with unusually fine masks on the rims.
Mid-18th century.
3¼ in. wide.

M. Hakim

In England the taking of snuff had been secondary to smoking until the 18th century. But by the middle of the century 'snuffing was a practice common to all ranks of Society and had many ardent votaries amongst the fair sex . . .'[9] From the accounts of the Gore family at Bourton, it appears at least a pound of snuff weekly on an average was consumed in that family. At that time (1753) the fashionable snuffs were sold at 8/- to 32/- a pound. The great snuffing period was from 1750 to 1785. During this time corn mills were converted to grind snuff and it reached such a

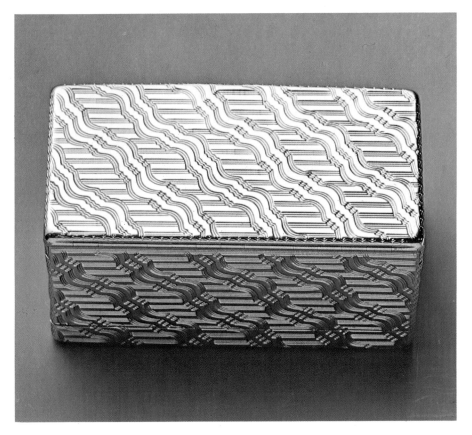

A double-opening snuff-box, decorated with panels of engine turning, by Jean Ducrollay.
Paris, 1754.
3⅛ in. wide.

Wartski, London

pitch that the authorities, fearing a shortage of flour, legislated against it.[10] In 1782 William Cowper, the poet, in a letter to the Rev. John Newton wrote:

[10] ibid., p. 17.

> Says the pipe to the snuff box, I can't understand
> What the ladies and the Gentlemen see in your face,
> That you are in fashion all over the land,
> And I am so much fallen into disgrace.

This was to be England's main contribution in the field of expensive snuff-boxes; the later boxes, for the most part, emulated French designs or alternatively rigidly interpreted neo-classical design and colouring.

In France in the late 1740s the snuff-box changed shape; new fashions came in and enamel appeared as one of the salient features. At first it was used primarily to embellish floral motifs, and amongst the most attractive examples of this style are those decorated with peonies and anemones, the design raised in gold and then enamelled in naturalistic colours. These boxes are amongst the most attractive and distinguished ever produced. The Royal manufactory of porcelain at Sèvres had begun to reproduce imitation flowers in porcelain in 1748 – apparently first ordered by Madame de Pompadour in order to surprise her Royal lover with a bank of flowers in full bloom in mid-winter. In ornament it was a sign of the return to nature that was to become manifest everywhere. In the *corbeille* of Marie Joseph de Saxe, who was married in 1747, was included a box decorated with a hawthorn spray with enamelled leaves and diamond flowers: others were decorated with ears of corn, pansies and cherries. Lazare Duvaux,[11] the royal 'jeweller', noted in his day-book – the best record of current taste in Paris in the fields of furniture, porcelain and jewelled objects of vertu – that Hébast was producing snuff-boxes with roses, pinks, anemones, hyacinths and tulips.

[11] Duvaux, Lazare, *Livre-journal*, 2 vols, Paris, 1873.

About this time the first 'cagework' boxes appeared. As might be supposed, the lid, sides and base panels fitted into a skeletal gold oblong cage. This meant that a box could be more easily produced, and a particularly popular model could be almost mass-produced in its various component parts. Occasionally the retailer, who was not strictly allowed to do so, fitted his own panels either of lacquer or mother-of-pearl or under-glass miniatures into the cagework mounts. Under guild law this was illegal, but it was a rule which must have been frequently contravened. A cagework box in which the panels are of carved and stained mother-of-pearl set against an engraved gold ground, with subjects after Teniers, was made by the Paris box-maker Dominic-François Poitreau in 1759.

12 Evans, op. cit., p. 135.

13 le Corbeille, op. cit., p. 24.

Dutch subjects had been in vogue since 1738. De Beaumarchais' *Le Holland*, followed by *Les Amusements de la Holland* (1739) and *Lettres Hollandaises* (1737) prompted the introduction of Dutch peasant scenes after Teniers into French art.[12] In the *Comptes Royeaux*, 1758, there are snuff-boxes recorded as made for the Crown '*emaillées figures d'après Teniers*'. In 1760 three boxes are described as '*à figures flamandes*', but Dutch subjects didn't really correspond with current French taste and there is no doubt that this fashion was partly motivated by commercial rather than artistic reasons. However, during the height of its popularity Diderot exclaimed '*j'aime mieux la rusticité que la migniardise, je donnerois dix Watteaus pour un Teniers*'.

During the third quarter of the 18th century the French goldsmiths developed the technique of box-making in *quatre couleur* gold. Paris led the rest of Europe in this technique and all those who emulated it at a later date, especially the Swiss, could never reproduce the sculptural effect that the French achieved in such perfectly balanced colours of gold. The technique of decorating in vari-coloured gold had been in existence for some time, but it didn't come fully into fashion until the mid-1750s. The colour of the gold could be changed by mixing it with other metals. There were four basic colours which could be achieved: white, red, green and blue.[13] The exact mixture of the metals needed to achieve these colours is given in *Secrets concernant les arts et métiers*, published in 1790. White gold was basically silver to which various amounts of gold were added; green gold was also an alloy of gold and silver and depending on the balance of the mixture three colours could be made – *vert de pré, beau vert feuille mort* and *vert d'eau*. Red gold was produced by adding one part of copper to three parts of 24 carat gold: for blue gold arsenic or steel-filings were added to the precious metal.

Perhaps one of the greatest exponents of this technique as well as being one of the great French box-makers of the 18th century, was Jean Ducrollay. Much of his work dates from this period and although he worked in many other techniques his *quatre couleur* boxes display a sculptural quality unsurpassed at any later period.

By 1760 the more fashionable box-makers had restricted the use of four-coloured gold decoration to the more minor areas of decoration; the borders from now on advertised this technique. From then until the Revolution, thirty years later, there were predominantly two types of box which were fashionable. In the first group under-glass gouache miniatures took the place of enamelled panels. Portrait boxes had been made since the King's portrait had adorned the earliest diplomatic presentation boxes, but now nearly all the portrait boxes were made in cheaper media and the one artist whose work was almost exclusively mounted in gold as an appreciation of his standing was Louis-Nicolas van Blarenberghe (1716–1794), who was followed by his son Henri-Joseph, and who painted in the manner of his father. Van Blarenberghe's subject matter included views of châteaux, pastoral scenes after Boucher, and *fêtes champêtres*. A circular box which may have been used either for powder or for snuff, the lid of which is inset with a view very much in the manner of van Blarenberghe, but unfortunately unsigned, is painted with a view of Lyon showing the Place Bellecour with the monument to Louis XIV erected in 1688 by Desjardins, which was destroyed in the Revolution. The box is dated 1788.[14]

14 A bronze reduction of this monument, dated 1726, was sold at Sothebys: see Catalogue of June 10, 1969, lot 76.

However, the 'return to antiquity' that occurred in the early 1760s changed the ornamentation and shape of snuff-boxes. Grecian taste had become a mania, everything in Paris was '*à la Grecque*', wrote Grimm in 1763 – exteriors and interiors of buildings, furniture, fabrics, jewellery. 'Our ladies have their hair done *à la grecque*, our *petits maîtres* would be ashamed to carry a snuff-box that was not *à la grecque*'.[15] The border decorations of naturalistic flowers and animals were replaced by Greek key patterns or laurel wreaths. Gone too were the rococo shapes. From now on the conventional shapes were either oval or oblong with canted corners, to allow for classical columnar supports, whilst the enamelling

15 Honour, Hugh, *Neo-Classicism*, Pelican Books, London, 1968, p. 27.

A topographical snuff-box with a view of
Place Bellcour in Lyons, in the manner of
van Blarenberghe.
Paris, 1788.
3 in. diameter.
Sotheby & Co.

itself changed in a subtle way. The inevitable scene from antiquity on the
lid was set into gold borders whilst other types were enclosed within
translucent enamel borders which showed engine-turning to advantage
beneath, or alternatively simple scenes in the *basse-taille* technique.[16]
The high-water mark of neo-classicism, before the Revolution, can be
seen in boxes set with *grisaille* miniatures by Jacques-Joseph de Gault
(1735–*c.* 1812). His subject matter is almost exclusively confined to
reproducing classical Bacchic friezes in miniature *en grisaille*. Early

[16] *Basse taille*: in this technique the metal
plate is routed away as in the *champlevé*
technique, but is carefully worked in
intaglio, so that the varying depths of the
carving can be seen through the translucent
enamel to achieve a three-dimensional
effect.

A neo-classical box by Drais of Paris, set
with *grisaille* miniatures by de Gault.
Paris, 1770.
3¾ in. wide.
Sotheby & Co.

A typical early box by Joseph-Etienne Blerzy, with borders of simulated rubies and pearls.
Paris, 1777.
3½ in. wide.

Sotheby & Co.

examples of his work were specially executed for the célebrated goldsmith Pierre-François Drais and are set into the box shown, which is dated 1770.

The change in styles during the twenty years preceding the Revolution can best be traced in the works of Joseph-Etienne Blerzy. He was a prolific maker, and some of his earlier pieces are inscribed '*au Petit Dunkerque*' on the lip of the box to denote that they were retailed through the Queen's jeweller, Granchez. His boxes made between 1775 and 1791 fall into two types. In the first his use of bright and distinctively coloured enamels is

A diamond-set snuff-box by Joseph-Etienne Blerzy.
Paris, 1785.
3¼ in. wide.

Sotheby & Co.

easily recognisable; vivid coloured leaves are set against a matt gold ground. Another of his favourite devices was to simulate small rubies and seed pearls in enamel. His later type of box which dates from the mid-1780s is more neo-classical and 'English' in style (trade had re-opened between the two countries in 1786) with arabesques against a dark blue ground. There is no doubt that the influence of the Sèvres porcelain factory still hung heavily over the production of boxes in the choice of palette and ornament.

With the flight to Varennes in 1791 revolutionary decoration began: griffins, eagles, sirens and fasces – the latter symbolising the law – and the oak leaf of civic virtue replace the less severe 'antique' motifs. The death knell to many of the goldsmiths and box-makers in Paris was rung in September of 1789 when the King himself, against the wishes of the National Assembly, melted the entire '*Argenterie de la Couronne*'[17] to help the country out of its financial difficulties. Producing, as they were, the most extravagant of all luxury objects for the nobility it was quite obvious at the time of the Revolution that it would be some little time before there would be anything approaching the same demand. France reverted to the manufacture of boxes in cheaper media – especially in pressed wood and papier mâché – whilst some of her goldsmiths left for the centres in Switzerland and London.

For nearly a century the French goldsmiths had dictated fashion to the rest of Europe. But now there were other centres specialising in different styles of box which were to become very popular.

Hardstone Boxes

Germany, during the 18th century, was rich in harstone deposits and much use of these was made by her box-makers. The mines of Bohemia and Silesia could provide any number of types of quartz. The most common were agate, carnelian, jasper and bloodstone. Rock-crystal was popular in France for making *boîtes à bonbons*. There was a ready trade in hardstone boxes, especially to the Grand Tourist; geological specimens were an integral part of the collector's cabinet in the 18th century in England and the enormous quantity of gold-mounted hardstone boxes, quite often

[17] Evans, op. cit., p. 115, footnote 2.

A French enamelled powder-box, probably
by Jean-Noël Gourdin.
Paris, 1784.
2½ in. diameter.

An unusual Neuber of Dresden box, in
which the hardstones are set into a quartzite
core.
c. 1770.
3½ in. wide.

in jasper, to be found in this country suggests that every Grand Tourist on the Rhine came back with such a box in the late 18th century.

The most magnificent snuff-boxes made during this century came from Berlin and were made for Frederick II who probably used them as diplomatic presents. Of unusually large size they are made of chrysophase and are decorated with chinoiseries or architectural views in hundreds of different sized diamonds.

During the last quarter of the 18th century Dresden emerged as the prime centre for hardstone boxes. Again, appealing to the Grand Tourist (now to be found collecting cameos and intaglios in various hardstones in Naples and Rome) who might be tempted by a box made of different types of agate accompanied by an explanatory booklet, concealed in a hidden receptacle in the base, which identified each numbered example. These were the speciality of the factory of Johann Christian Neuber (1736–1808).[18] He had been appointed court jeweller in 1775, and one of his earlier boxes, set with a Meissen porcelain plaque, is made up of strips of vermilion and green agate set into a quartzite core. This is a rare technique; in most of the later boxes made for the tourist market the hardstone pieces were held by gold cloisons.

Also for the Grand Tourist, impressed by the mosaics in Naples, were workshops reproducing in miniature the most famous of them, particularly popular being animals, and in England, dogs. The workshops only made the mosaic panels; these were then sold either to local trinket makers or to merchants abroad. Some were incorporated into caskets and boxes in London. They were still being produced in the middle of the 19th century.

[18] For a fuller account of this maker's work see Walter Holzhausen's pamphlet, 'Johann Christian Neuber', Dresden, 1943: also the *Antique Collector*, London, March/April 1943.

A Neapolitan mosaic of a dog set into an English tortoise-shell snuff-box.
c. 1800.
3⅜ in. diameter.

M. Hakim

Living conditions were very different in the 18th century to those of today. Society had no great regard for domestic or personal hygiene. Houses were most insanitary. Lavatories were by no means in general use yet; even Versailles boasted no lavatory until the time of Louis XVI and then it was only for the use of the King and Queen.[19] Henry de Catt found the bad air and unsavoury conditions at Grüssan Monastery just as intolerable as Keyssler did at the Doges Palace in Venice.

Bathrooms too were lacking. The one that existed at Versailles was walled in and when it was discovered by chance was removed to Madame de Pompadour's park to serve as a basin for a fountain. Saint Simon records that Louis XIV only took baths when he was still in love, and at the levée the Roi Soleil simply wiped his face with a handkerchief drenched in scent; a courtier poured a few drops of rosewater and orange-flower water over the King's fingers to conclude his toilette. During the 17th century pomanders were used by the fashionable to dispel any unpleasant odours. These had evolved into vinaigrettes[20] by the 18th century, but were not produced on anything like a commercial scale until the early 19th century when personal hygiene found a champion in the English middle class. So between pomander and vinaigrette the nobility in Europe simply drenched themselves in scent and covered any defect with rouge and powder. The wardrobe of Count von Brühl, the Saxon Premier, contained no less than sixty-three scent flacons.

Scent was produced locally and marketed regionally during the 18th century; small quantities were therefore syphoned-off from the domestic

[19] von Boehn, M., *Modes and Manners*, vol. IV, p. 271.

[20] It was not until *c.* 1800 that the true vinaigrette appeared, fitted with a pierced inner lid to retain the piece of scent-drenched sponge. Until then smaller versions of the snuff-box had been used.

A French late-Renaissance pomander with six segments.
c. 1600.
3⅞ in. high.
Parke-Bernet Galleries Inc., New York

supply into the scent flask. There is no doubt that the porcelain factories were in a monopolistic position in the middle of the century: like glass, which was used at a later period, the porcellaneous paste could be simply moulded and decorated, whereas gold flasks, as well as those made of copper and enamel, had to be beaten out of sheet metal – a more lengthy procedure until the die-process came in in Sheffield at the end of the century.

Yet there are some very attractive gold, enamel and hardstone flasks

An English double scent bottle, carved from agate, in the form of a young shepherd holding a lamb.
c. 1760.
3½ in. high.

Victoria and Albert Museum

which still survive today. One of these, very much inspired by a porcelain original, shows a young shepherd holding a lamb. It is English and dates from *c.* 1760.

Another slightly smaller and earlier piece made in Paris during the rococo period is interesting since the goldsmith had a greater opportunity to work 'in the round' than with a snuff-box where any really imaginative design is united by the conventional shape.

A gold *repoussé* scent bottle on a cornelian seal-set base.
Mid-18th century.
2½ in. long.
Victoria and Albert Museum

Patch boxes, or *boîtes à mouches* as they were called, were generally oblong and a little shallower than snuff-boxes; in the latter part of the 18th century they got a little more squat when they were fitted with compartments for patches and rouge, with a piece of looking-glass in the lid, and completed with a gum brush. This was used to dab the gum onto the little pieces of taffeta which were applied to the faces of both men and women throughout the century and drew attention to the facial features of the wearers. Women also applied them on their bosoms to exaggerate the whiteness of the skin. The patches were often cut out in different shapes and colours. At the height of the fashion patches are known to have been applied to less public parts of the female anatomy.

As in the 'language of faces', a code existed which was used by the wearer as a guide to her character. All depended on the position of the patch; De Resbecq, *Bibliothèque des Dames*,[21] lists the various positions. *La Passionnée* tended to wear them at the corner of the eye, whilst the less forward woman would wear it between the mouth and chin. These are only two of many permutations.

Etiquette dictated that gentlemen with powdered hair were required to wear patches just like the ladies and in their case powder and patches were used to match their age. Both old men and women alike attempted to reproduce the bloom of youth by powdering their faces, heavily

[21] Amsterdam (1765). As quoted by Snowman, op. cit., p. 40.

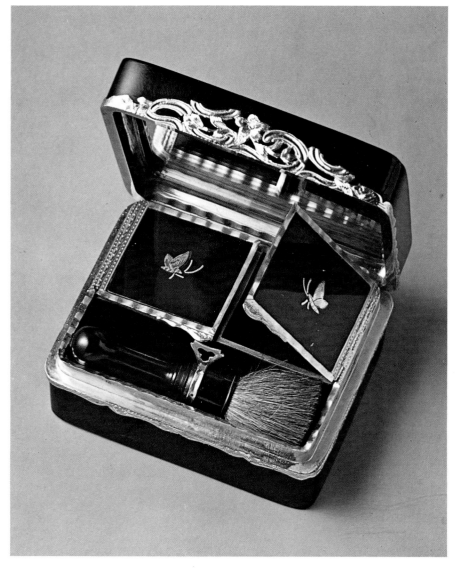

Left
A French patch box by M. Philippe, shown open with the gum brush, two compartments and looking glass.
Paris, 1758.
2½ in. long.

Wartski, London

[22] von Boehn, op. cit., vol. IV, p. 246.

rouging their cheeks and wore 'amber scented perukes' and patches.[22] In the wake of the patch box, usually in ivory and of elongated form, came the toothpick case. One of these, made during the Regency, is fitted with gaming discs.

Children applying patches to all parts of their body, a detail from 'Jeû d'enfants á Toilette', after Coypel, dated 1731.

Mrs Viva King

Chatelaines[23] in their most elaborate form really came into being in the middle of the 18th century and their form hardly changed until they went out of fashion around 1800. A series of decorated panels chained together were suspended from a belt hook and supported a watch, decorated *en suite*, which in turn was flanked by subsidiary chains for the crank key, fob seal and other toys and trinkets. Illustrated is a lady's chatelaine of this type (probably made in Birmingham), enamelled with vases of flowers and hung with various trinkets, the seal and order of which are of slightly later date. Émilie is shown wearing such a chatelaine hung with two fob seals and decorated with English neo-classical portrait medallions against a chocolate ground in the posthumous fantasy of Voltaire and Émilie by J. C. Mannlich.[24] It is possible to date ladies' chatelaines closely since the craftsmen who decorated snuff-boxes, usually stamped with the date letter, also decorated chatelaines. However, the name on the

[23] The prime function of the chatelaine was originally to support the pocket-watch; since watches form a subject in themselves they have been omitted from this book.

[24] In the collection of the Earl of Rosebery. Illustrated in Mitford, Nancy, *Voltaire in Love*, Hamish Hamilton, London, 1957, frontispiece.

A gentleman's gilt-metal chatelaine, flanked by two ladies' chatelaines hung with etuis, one in pinchbeck, the other in gold. 1770–80.
Right-hand chatelaine: 7½ in. (overall length).
Private collection and Sotheby & Co.

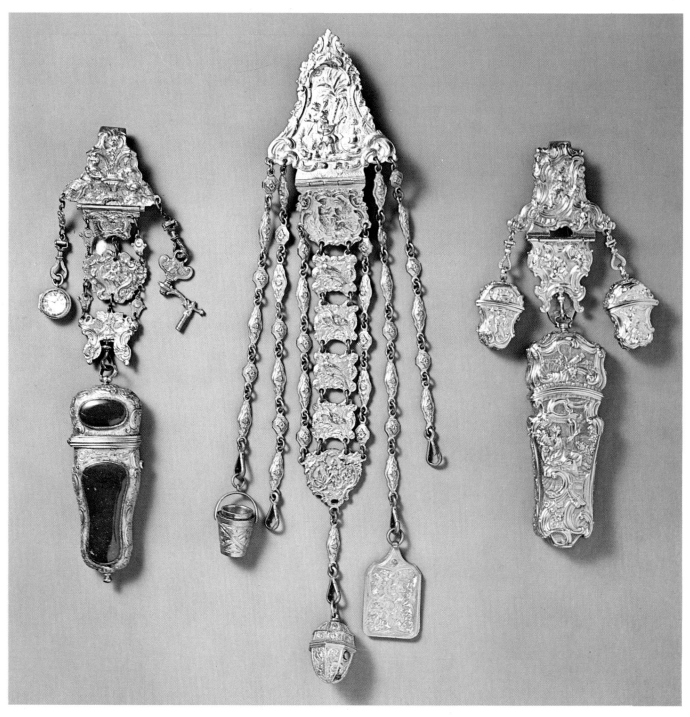

Two English chatelaines, one with neo-classical miniatures after Moser, the other, which is earlier in date, with still life motifs. The watch movement is signed *John Scott, London.*
c. 1780 and 1770.
6⅛ and 7⅝ in long.

M. Hakim

dial of the watch might well be that of the retailer; a London address was the best provenance for mechanical objects – especially watches or guns – during the last quarter of the 18th century and both English provincial makers and Continental producers fraudulently inscribed their pieces with 'London' to take advantage of a higher price.

The gentleman's chatelaine was of a different form. It was longer and usually supported a cluster of fob-seals and toys. Two were worn suspended on each thigh to conceal the openings of the flap on the breeches; the

fashionable man was expected to make a lively jingling noise when he entered a room, and charms and seals were carefully chosen to attain the greatest audible effect. This art of seal and trinket wearing was taken so seriously during this period that for those who were deficient tuition could be received at a number of schools in Paris.[25]

In the 1780s cut-steel chatelaines for men, such as those produced by the factories of Matthew Boulton in Birmingham, were much sought after and very expensive on the Continent. At the height of their popularity Marie Antoinette was painted by Adolf Ulrik Wertmüller (1785) accompanied by her children and wearing a pair of probably English chatelaines, in the masculine manner, on each thigh.[26]

The French Revolution imposed a simpler form of costume. The only outward show of extravagance that a young fashionable gentleman could afford to wear publicly was an ornamented waistcoat; chatelaines became simpler in design so that by the turn of the century they had evolved into a gold mesh band or a cut of silk ribbon to support the fob-seals. Watches were no longer worn in an exposed position by either of the sexes. This was the only time that cut-steel – so popular in swords and buckles – had made its mark on objects of vertu. However, it survived in England and Germany in a more moderate form until later.[27]

Chatelaines also served as supports for étuis during the second half of the 18th century. Most of these would appear to be English and made of 'pinchbeck' (named after its inventor, Christopher Pinchbeck the Elder), in which the gold-substitute is 90% copper and 10% zinc,[28] reputed not only to look like gold but to smell like it also. That shown contains a collection of instruments including a snuff-spoon, ivory *aide mémoire*,

[25] von Boehn, op. cit., vol. IV, pp. 225–6.

[26] ibid., p. 241.
[27] For the extraordinary account of *Bijoux en fonte de Berlin*, see D'Allemagne (see Bibliography) p. 42 and plate XVIII; this would appear to be one of the few occasions on which a new fashion has been imposed on a society purely for political ends.

Cut steel remained popular in England until the third-quarter of the century; there were several manufacturers with a wide range of products at the 1851 Exhibition.

[28] The percentages as recorded by le Corbeille, op. cit., p. 62. For further details of Christopher and Edward Pinchbeck, see Benton, E., Exhibition of Gilt Metal and Enamel at The Art Gallery, Royal Leamington Spa, October 1967, *Catalogue*, p. 4.

An English cagework *nécessaire*, fitted with scent bottles, tablet, knife and spoon.
c. 1760.
2 in. high.

Sotheby & Co.

folding knife and scissors. The enamel suspended to the left is a miniature toy watch.

Not really portable and probably intended for use on a dressing table is an English nécessaire. These were made in varying sizes and contained different combinations of fittings. They were produced around 1770 and must have come from the same workshop. Many have amatory inscriptions in French on the rims, in gold against white enamel; quite often they are mis-spelt. The gold cagework encloses backed agate.

Other functional accessories include bodkin cases and sealing-wax cases. The first was to aid the embroideress, of whom there were many in England in the middle of the century when the fashion for sprays of flowers in ornament set everybody making court petticoats. French ladies, on the other hand, felt less inclined to pursue such occupations, even after 1762 when Rousseau incited the lazier strata of society when he exclaimed 'every idle citizen is a rogue . . . learn a trade'. However, the publishing of Diderot's *L'Encyclopédie* showing numerous instruments and tools brought them into fashion in ornament and by the end of the century the makers of étuis and nécessaires were cramming more and more miniature implements into their products.

The most likely explanation why so many étuis have survived is that a great quantity were made at the time. The middle-class woman in the 18th century lived a very retired life; any social intercourse outside the home existed only for men. Sewing and needlework provided one of the few diversions and the fashion for 'receiving' in the mornings allowed for admiration of an expensive receptacle for one's implements.

A sealing-wax case in gold, with another enamelled in white.
Paris, 1777.
A bodkin case decorated with panels of girls.
Swiss, late 18th century.
4½ to 4⅞ in. long.

Sotheby & Co.

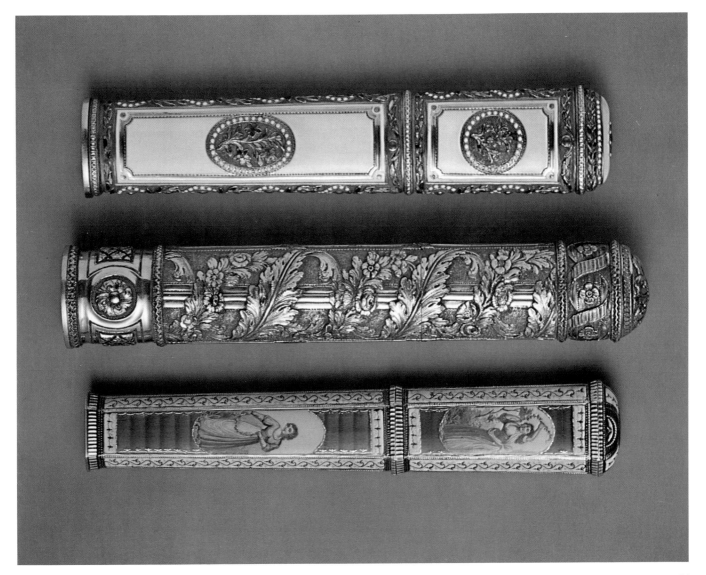

In the second half of the 18th century ladies started to use long thin canes with gold handles which they carried 'majestically in the middle'.[29] Mercier in 1782 wrote in *Tableau de Paris*, 'it is not for them a vain ornament, they have more need of them than men because of their bizarre high heels which give them height yet deprive them of the ability to walk'.

The cane had been in and out of fashion since the 16th century. During the late 17th century the better quality ones had ivory pommels decorated in piqué, but it was not until the second quarter of the 18th century that elaborate handles in gold and enamel, silver or porcelain, were available. There were basically two types. Firstly, the simple pommel with flared ferrule and convex top. The second was of *tao* shape. The latter was particularly suited to rococo ornament and in gold was more durable than its counterpart in porcelain – hence a good reason for the goldsmith's enthusiasm for this type. This shape lingered on in Germany where its form adapted well to hardstone sphinx-like creatures.

In the simpler form of stick the decoration closely followed that on snuff-boxes, and most of the surviving examples were made in *quatre couleur* gold, in preference to enamel, for durability. Yet there were refinements. Allemagne records that runners in the 18th century could carry canes with bottles of cordial in the pommel to give 'new strength to the exhausted athlete'; whilst *L'Almanach sous Verre* for 1785 announced Cassemiche's invention of a candle set into a cane handle, complete with reflector, which would be of use to the nocturnal wanderer.

[29] D'Allemagne, op. cit., pp. 78–9.

An English gold cagework and agate corkscrew, and a Dutch diamond merchant's gold corn tongs, and shovel for diamonds, maker E.A.
Corkscrew, *c*. 1760, 3 11/16 in. long.
Tongs, *c*. 1775, 3 1/4 in. long.
Private collection

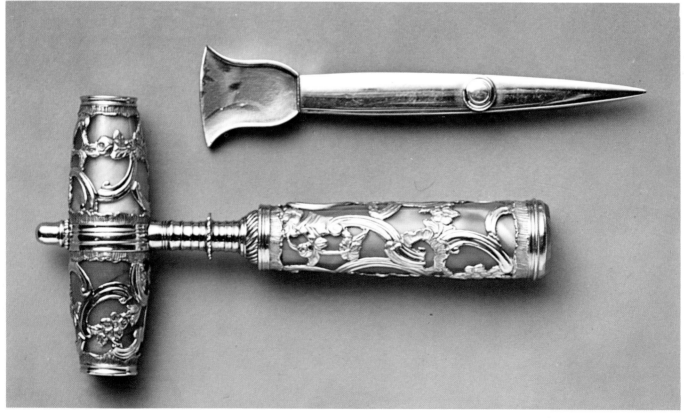

Carnets de Bal and Aides Mémoire

In the 18th century *tablettes* were one of the few accessories which one could give as presents. In 1714 Louis XIV had given the Queen of Spain, amongst other objects of vertu, a tablette worth 1200 livres. 'Tablettes' were so-called since they were simple leaves of ivory on which notes could be written. These were contained in a decorative case. Those which could be taken out of the case were usually for use as *carnets de bal*. It was customary for the young girl to inscribe on these the names of her intended partners for each dance at the beginning of the Ball and to refer to it to avoid compromise. *Aides mémoire*, on the other hand, were set in a binding and at a later date had paper leaves. The advantage of ivory leaves was that writing in lead pencil could be easily erased with a damp cloth.

A young Victorian girl consulting her *carnet de bal*, and surrounded by hopeful admirers; from *La Vie Parisienne*.[30]

[30] *La Vie Parisienne*, 13 March, 1886, p. 147.

succès. — Tout est retenu, avant même son entrée au bal. On s'y prend huit jours à l'avance, et six semaines pour le cotillon. S'embrouille dans ses écritures, et la valse appartient au malin qui affirme catégoriquement qu'elle lui a été promise

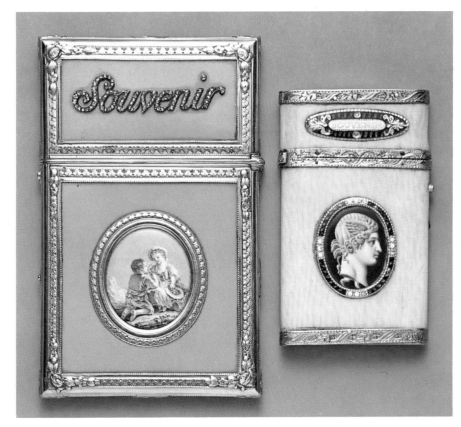

A French *carnet de bal*, the inscription set with diamonds.
Paris, 1768.
3½ in. long.
An English neo-classical *carnet de bal*, in ivory, enamelled after Moser.
London, *c.* 1785.
2⅞ in. long.

Sotheby & Co.

Painted Enamels

The discovery of a practical way of producing porcelain in the early 18th century meant that for the first time household objects such as candlesticks and domestic utensils as well as portable objects such as snuff-boxes could be produced in this medium. Before this the goldsmiths and silversmiths had monopolised this field, but here was a cheap and attractive alternative. One of the earliest factories, and undoubtedly one of the most successful, was at Meissen in Saxony. Their first table wares entirely of porcelain and decorated with painted scenes emerged in the 1730s; shortly after this the factory's output expanded into related wares including snuff-boxes and candlesticks. As the reputation of the Meissen factory grew, so the enamelling workshops which could produce a cheaper type of snuff-box expanded. The advantage which the enamel manufacturers held over the porcelain producers can be found in the actual process of manufacture. The factories engaged in enamelling could make any number of 'enamel blanks' – that is boxes, decorative plaques, watchbacks or utensils in copper, simply covered in a coat of white enamel. These could be stock-piled in the workshops until they were needed, then be decorated by a painter in any style fashionable at that moment. Since the shapes of boxes hardly changed from decade to decade this proto-

A Fromery workshops box in the form of a sedan chair.
Mid-18th century.
4 in. high.

Sotheby & Co.

assembly-line process gave the enamel producers an edge over the porcelain factories in the cheaper markets.

The Fromery workshops in Berlin were perhaps the most important and prolific producers of enamelled wares in the early part of the century. Their works are easily distinguishable from those of their competitors. Their boxes are decorated with silvered or gilded relief ornament (sometimes with green added) against a white ground.

The workshops had been founded by Pierre Fromery, but it was his son Alexander who perfected and put into production this highly individual style of box.[1] Whereas most of the mounts on painted enamel boxes were made of gilded copper in the 18th century, the Fromery workshops when making a good-quality box mounted it in silver. This was particularly pleasing when combined with silvered relief ornament. Of all the German 18th century snuff-boxes to be found in collections today, it is those of the Fromery workshops that stand out as consistently maintaining a high degree of quality quite often to be found wanting in the work of contemporaries.

As the century progressed the German enamelling workshops declined and became more imitative. The Augsburg workshops had retained not a little status from the early part of the century when their painted enamelled vessels were the finest in Europe, but there is no doubt that they were seriously affected by the success of the English factories' export trade.[2] From the late 1740s onwards one of their main products was the cheap box made basically to amuse. The Du Paquier porcelain factory in Austria had made boxes painted with playing cards in the 1730s,[3] and it was this type of design which the enamellers copied. Other types include boxes

[1] le Corbeille, op. cit., pp. 72–4.

[2] A large Augsburg casket, the lid reminiscent of English painted casket lids of the early 1750s, and mounted in ormolu, was sold at Sothebys, November 27, 1967, see *Catalogue*, lot 148.

[3] For an account of gambling in the 18th century see von Boehn, op. cit., p. 293; 'At Ratisbon a lady was driven from the card-table only by the pains of labour . . .'.

An Augsburg painted enamel egg *bonbonnière* with gold mounts.
c. 1720–30.
2⅜ in. long.

M. Hakim

A commemorative snuff-box with a portrait of Frederick the Great from an engraving by J. G. Wille (1715–1808), after the painting by Antoine Pesne (1683–1787).
c. 1760.
3⅛ in. long.

Victoria and Albert Museum

A snuff-box enamelled with stanzas from a popular air.
Mid-18th century.
3 in. long.

Sotheby & Co.

of very shallow form painted in black and white in the form of envelopes, those with *trompe-l'œil* panels, extracts from letters, or stanzas from popular tunes. But by 1770 the manufacture of painted enamel boxes in Germany was rendered unviable on anything like a commercially competitive scale by the success of the porcelain factories, by the exploitation of the great quantities of attractive hardstones to be found in Germany which were used in the manufacture of boxes, and lastly by the influx of cheap boxes from England. However, the final type which can be distinguished as German emerged just before and during the Seven Years War (1757–1763) and was a vehicle for spreading propaganda for the Prussian cause.

Frederick the Great was fighting this war on several fronts and was remarkably successful against great odds. His victories were immodestly blazed across the lids of boxes, sometimes with his portrait, sometimes with a battle scene. The quality of painting on many of these 'war-time' productions is not of a high standard compared with contemporary English boxes, but one of the reasons for this was that many of these commemorative boxes were available to the general public within a few days of the actual event illustrated on the lid so as to take advantage of the buying potential generated by patriotic fervour. One of these, depicting the battle of Leuthen, 5th December 1757, is dated a week after the event.[4]

Contemporary with this latter series are the German and Austrian 'portrait' boxes which are of unusually high quality. The sitter was usually shown half-length against either an olive-green ground or a liver-coloured ground on the inside of the lid. Some of these were by Daniel Chodowiecki, who was Frederick's chief designer and engraver.

With the exception of the Fromery productions, there are often very few indications as to where many of these boxes were made. To make it even more difficult, many enamel workshops followed the practice of the porcelain factories and put out much of their work to painters working independently of the factory. These were known as *Hausmalerei*. Some of the painters on porcelain have been identified;[5] it is perhaps easier to distinguish between the different hands and personal styles on larger porcelain objects such as jugs and tankards. Unfortunately, comparatively few decorators of enamel boxes have been identified. Even the author of a

[4] Hayward, J. F., *Apollo*, London, April 1945.

[5] For the most comprehensive account see Pazaurek (in Bibliography).

German *Hausmaler* snuff-box by the painter of the life of Tobias and other biblical scenes.
Mid-18th century.
3¼ in. wide.
Victoria and Albert Museum

A Russian enamel tea caddy in the style of Fromery of Berlin.
c. 1745.
5½ in. high.

Sotheby & Co.

Below
Dutch set of silver-gilt cutlery, with painted enamel handles.
Early 18th century.
6⅞ in. (overall length).

Parke-Bernet Galleries Inc., New York

particularly amusing series of biblical boxes remains unknown. These can be easily recognised by the elongated form of the box and the choice of a biblical subject – often the story of Tobias – and also a palette with greens and orange-red predominating. There is, however, a possibility that the ornament was taken from earlier Brussels tapestry designs and that this group originated in the Low Countries and not in Germany. A knife and fork from the former, made in the early part of the century, are painted with mythological figures and fruit.

Russia in the 18th century could claim few indigenous workmen. Most of the few enamelled objects which survive from this period show obvious foreign influence. In the earlier part of the century the Dutch influence on such objects as two-handled bowls is evident;[6] by the middle of the century it is the influence of the Fromery workshops which is more evident; the tea caddy shown displays this inspiration but the quality of the decoration in which the silvering is wide and 'putty-like' cannot be compared favourably with the original. It is most likely that it was executed by a German craftsman working in the foreign artisans' quarter in Moscow.

[6] These are in contrast to the more common *cloisonné* wares of the mid-17th century: the technique of painting in enamel was probably introduced to Russia by Peter the Great after his visit to Holland, since the few extant examples follow closely the Dutch originals.

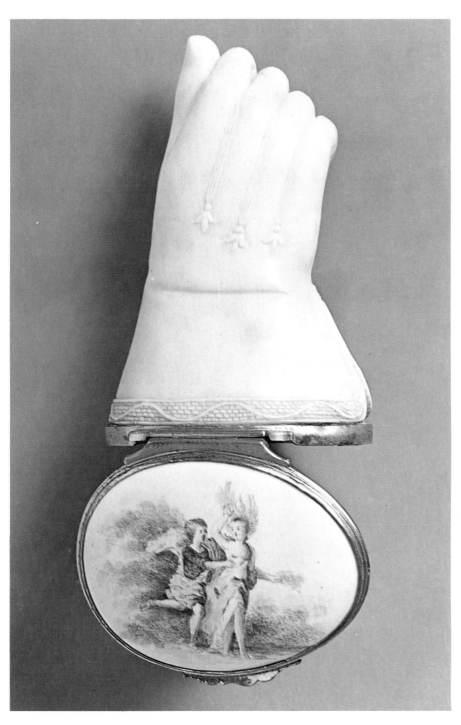

An ivory 'glove' box with an enamelled lid depicting Daphne and Apollo. German, mid-18th century. 3¼ in. long.

M. Hakim

Both Peter the Great and the Empress Catherine had made great efforts to stimulate the skilled crafts by enticing workmen from abroad. Yet examples of enamelled objects and objects of vertu are not as evident in Russia during the 18th century as they are in the rest of Europe; this again is probably due to the pre-eminence of the silversmiths (niello-decorated silver was very popular then and was to remain so for at least another century) and to the fact that, as in France, a middle-class such as could be found in England did not exist.

English painted enamels

Until comparatively recently English enamels had been lumped together and indiscriminately described as Battersea by the layman. But although Bernard Rackham[7] differentiated between Battersea and the rest it was not until 1966 that Dr Watney and Mr Charleston published their findings on the earlier period.[8]

The Battersea factory, on the south bank of the Thames, flourished for only three years between 1753 and 1756 and was regarded by most students of 18th century enamels as having introduced transfer-printing as well as being the first English concern to produce painted enamels in any quantity. However, it is now known that the really important enamel-producing area centred on Staffordshire and together with Birmingham was making enamelled boxes and wares in the late 1740s before the foundation of the Battersea factory. Transfer-printing, an English invention, made it possible for boxes and objects of vertu to be mass-produced almost mechanically without the aid of a painter. However, there was a

[7] *Catalogue of the Schreiber Collection* (see Bibliography).

[8] Watney, B., and Charleston, R., *Transactions of the English Ceramic Circle*, vol. VI, part II, 1966.

A Birmingham casket with coloured transfer prints after Watteau, the sides decorated with flowers.
c. 1754.
8 in. wide.
Sotheby & Co.

A gilt-metal box, probably made in Birmingham after the Meissen originals.
c. 1740–5.
3¼ in. long.

Private collection

A snuff-box painted with a portrait of a
young girl.
c. 1755.
3¼ in. wide.

Sotheby & Co.

43

disadvantage in that transfer-printed enamels looked very austere alongside those enriched with a layer of paint.

Birmingham was the main centre for the manufacture of 'enamel blanks'. The towns of Bilston and Wednesbury in South Staffordshire have always been associated with enamelling, but as yet few definite types or styles have been associated with either place. This is possibly because during the middle of the 18th century the various components were made in different towns – blanks in one centre and gilt mounting frames in another. Indeed, the whole industry really stemmed from the gilt metal workshops, where the first boxes were made. After a short time they began to incorporate a painted enamel lid. This was in the early 1740s. It wasn't until the end of the decade that enamelling became the more important element.[9] Birmingham had the reputation of being the 'Toyshop of Europe'[10] with a large slice of the export trade and there would seem to be very little doubt that they also supplied the components for the Battersea York Road factory. From the registers available it is quite evident that there were many more enamellers living in the Staffordshire and Birmingham areas than in London. And it was to Birmingham that the Irish engraver John Brooks came to apply, on the 10th September 1751, for the patent-rights on his new idea of transfer-printing on enamels and ceramics. In this, his first unsuccessful application, the technique which was to revolutionise the ceramic and enamel industries was described as follows . . . 'John Brooks of Birmingham . . . has by great study, application and expense found out a method of printing, impressing and reversing upon enamel and china from engraved, etched and mezzotint plates, and from

Right
A Battersea enamel plaque painted with the arms of the Anti-Gallican Society, of which Alderman Janssen had been a past-president.
c. 1755.
4 in. long.
A Battersea plaque transfer-printed with Andromeda, after a print attributed to Ravenet.
c. 1754.
4½ in. wide.
Sotheby & Co.

[9] Benton, op. cit., p. 3.

[10] The word 'toy' or 'toie' seems to be a variant on 'tie' or 'tye', meaning a small metal box or casket in early 18th century South Staffordshire usage: see Benton, op. cit., p. 3.

Below
A pair of cylindrical tea caddies, the spoon with silver-gilt handle.
Birmingham, *c.* 1755–60.
7½ in. high.
Sotheby & Co.

cuttings on wood and metal, impressions of History, Portraits, Land-scapes, Foliages, Coats of Arms, Cyphers, Letters, Decorations, and other Devices. That the said art is entirely new and of his own invention . . .'.

Two years later Brooks moved from Birmingham to London where he became manager of the Battersea factory which had been founded by Sir Stephen Theodore Jannsen. Perhaps after his unsuccessful application in Birmingham he felt that London would prove a more sophisticated and appreciative centre for his transfer-printed objects of vertu. There is no doubt that London retailers had been buying Birmingham productions in other fields, only to sign the finished article with their own signature[11] and a London address, and there is a possibility that Brooks and Jannsen felt that it would be more profitable to obtain components from Birmingham, decorate the blanks in London and to break into the market there. Whilst in London, Brooks made two further unsuccessful petitions; in these he claimed that he would use the process to print on glass as well as china and enamel. The Battersea factory went bankrupt in 1756.

The best indication of the output and scope of the factory can be gleaned

[11] This was very much the case in the production of fire-arms during the 18th century. In Europe the two most important centres were London and Paris. Makers in Birmingham and Liége often signed their works with spurious addresses.

Birmingham snuff-box inscribed in Russian: 'God save Elizabeth I, Empress of all the Russias'; other inscriptions commemorate the battle of Kunersdorf, 12th August 1759, fought between Frederick the Great and a Russian and Austrian army under Saltnikof.
3¼ in. wide.

Eric Benton collection

from two advertisements. The first appeared in the *London Daily Advertiser* to announce the sale of the contents of Jannsen's house in February 1756 and lists 'a quantity of beautiful enamels, coloured and uncoloured of the new manufactory carried on at York House, Battersea, and never yet exhibited to public view, consisting of Snuff Boxes of all sizes of great variety of Patterns'. After this are listed the other products including square and oval pictures 'of the Royal Family, History and other pleasing subjects, very proper ornaments for Cabinets of the Curious'. The list concludes with wine labels, watch-cases and toothpick-cases, and particular emphasis is laid on the fact that the metal mounts were 'double gilt'. No doubt the chief criticism of gilt-metal mounted boxes as opposed to gold was that constant handling rubbed off the thin layer of gilding.

The second advertisement describes the bankrupt stock for sale at York House. It is dated 9th June 1756. In this the types of object produced by the factory are described and also listed are the great variety of blanks, unfinished enamels and mounting frames which had not been used.

To make it even more difficult for the student today to distinguish between the transfer-printed productions of Battersea and Birmingham, many of the engraved copperplates were bought-up together with partly finished objects by Birmingham makers. However, it is possible to distinguish between the two types by careful examination of the decoration added after the printing process was completed. In Battersea the quality of the printing was the most admired aspect of the finished production and any added decoration took this into account; if enriched with colour it was thinly applied and very translucent. Yet in Birmingham the print was used as a guide line for the enamel painter and on many products the original print can hardly be seen beneath a thick impasto of enamel. The prints, mostly attributed to Ravenet, usually depict classical, mythological and allegorical subjects as well as portraits and religious subjects; but the latter were comparatively rare and were probably made for export and not for home consumption in such an actively Protestant country.

One of the finest plaques made was that for the Anti-Gallican Society and transfer-printed and painted with its arms. Sir Theodore Jannsen was one of the Society's presidents.

The rather baroque putti which decorate wine labels and represent the arts and sciences (also appearing on the sides of snuff-boxes), are typical of the Battersea factory; the fashion for representing technical processes dates from the publication of the first volume of Diderot's *L'Encyclopédie* – a glorification of tools and technical processes – in 1751.[12]

The early works of Birmingham on the other hand can be distinguished by their shape, size and type of decoration. There exists a group of fairly large painted caskets, caddies and boxes, most of which have French-inspired decoration, of *fêtes champêtres* after Lancret, Watteau and Boucher, on the lids painted in a fairly sketchy hand. The sides of this group are invariably painted with scattered groups of flowers – delicately coloured moss-roses with meticulously painted thorns and with butterflies and insects hovering around. These stand out as being the most realistic of all flower sprays in art since the Dutch still-lifes of the previous century. Yet English gardens were 'perhaps the most flowery gardens of Europe'.[13] Thomson's *Seasons*, published in 1746, had a marked effect on taste; every plant seemed to be included in his poems, perhaps the Birmingham artists were effected by the following lines:

> . . . nor jonquils
> of potent fragrance; nor gay spotted pinks;
> Nor, showered from every bush, the damask rose.

One of the most important manufacturers in the field of enamels in Birmingham was a certain John Taylor. His factory was certainly well established in 1756 and a decade later Lady Shelburne visited him and recorded her memories.[14] 'At Mr Taylor's we met again and he made and enamel'd a landscape on the top of a box before us which he afterwards gave me as a curiosity from my having seen it done. The method of doing

[12] Evans, op. cit., p. 139.

[13] ibid., p. 142.

[14] As quoted by Dr Watney, 'English Enamels', *Antiques International*, Michael Joseph, London, 1966, p. 291.

it is this: a stamping instrument managed only by one woman first impresses the picture on paper, which paper is then laid even upon a piece of which enamel and rubbed hard with a knife, or instrument like it, till it is marked upon the box. Then there is spread over it with a brush some metallic colour reduced to a fine powder which adheres to the moist part and, by putting it afterwards into an oven for a few minutes, the whole is completed by fixing the colour.' This was one of the first transfer processes used at Birmingham, the later and more usual one is when the copper plate is inked with enamel colour, the design printed on paper and then transferred on to enamel. Taylor also probably used the plates engraved by R. Hancock, the most famous of which is the 'Tea Party' which also appeared on Bow and Worcester porcelain.

As has already been mentioned the later history of English enamels, from 1760 until 1820, is rather hazy. It was a prolific period and there is no doubt that Birmingham had a large part to play in it. On the whole the later boxes decline in quality. This is especially noticeable with objects made post-1780.

The two other towns which were famous for enamels were Wednesbury and Bilston. Of the former very little is known except that it is thought that the group of enamels decorated in white on a brilliant blue ground come from there. Bilston was certainly more prolific and to this centre are ascribed the 'form' boxes, made for snuff, sweets and occasionally for patches, often in imitation of Meissen with animals such as the leopard, and on the lid a hunting scene. Savage animals are much rarer than the more common canary boxes which were made in all sizes. Together with the repoussé scent bottles, these were emulating the German originals in an attempt to undercut the price of similar pieces in porcelain. The Chelsea factory had been manufacturing scent bottles, 'smelling-bottles', Etwees (étuis) and trinkets for watches (mounted in gold and unmounted) since at least 1754,[15] and the success of the South Staffordshire bottles can possibly be attributed to the fact that enamel on copper was less fragile than porcelain in objects of such small scale. Most of these 'form'-bottles or boxes are chipped – each apex being the most vulnerable part – but they were, even so, less fragile than the porcelain originals from which most of the designs were taken.

[15] *Cat. Schreiber Collection*, op. cit., part 1.

A leopard's head *bonbonnière*.
c. 1770.
3 in. wide.

Sotheby & Co.

48

Above
Staffordshire *bonbonnières.*
c. 1755–75.
1½–3 in. wide.

Sotheby & Co.

A Bilston enamel etui painted with a portrait of Miss Day, afterwards Lady Fenhoulet, after a painting by Reynolds. 4⅛ in. long.

Sotheby & Co.

Although the Staffordshire manufacturers held a fairly large percentage of the market in boxes and trinkets, they were perhaps less successful when they diversified their class of product into larger household utensils. The earlier examples mostly took the form of caskets, large circular powder boxes of the type produced in Birmingham (some containing caddies), and were probably commercially quite successful. This was because they had little competition from the silversmiths or porcelain factories, but when they started producing candlesticks and such household objects as water

A pair of Staffordshire enamel candlesticks. 10½ in. high.

Sotheby & Co.

50

jugs and clocks they were attempting to invade a new type of market already monopolised by the other crafts. Various technical problems existed. Whereas it was quite simple for a box-maker to produce his enamel blank, on an unusually large scale, for a casket, it was more difficult for him to beat out a piece of copper into the form of a jug or perfume-burner. In this he was required to achieve almost the same degree of skill as a silversmith and furthermore had to make absolutely certain that the enamel coating was spread evenly over an undulating surface before passing it on to the decorator. Having reached this stage it was decorated in the conventional way using standard prints; many workshops would appear not to have been in close touch with artistic designers since the same landscapes or motifs that appear on snuff-boxes appear on larger candlesticks, yet in small scale. However, in the urn-shaped perfume-burner the painting is freely drawn.

These large-scale objects form the rarest group within the subject of English painted enamels for the very reason that their attempt to compete commercially with examples in other materials was limited to certain

Right
A Staffordshire urn-shaped perfume burner.
c. 1775.
9½ in. high.

Sotheby & Co.

types of object – most of these like candlesticks and perfume-burners needed to be heat resistant – and possibly a combination of copper and enamel fared better than porcelain if exposed to a naked flame, which might happen if a candle burnt down too far; and it is possible that most of the really unusual models were specially commissioned. Consequently few table utensils apart from candlesticks, mustard and pepper pots and mugs were produced in England.

It was different, however, in Vienna where the workshops of the von Jüngers flourished from *c.* 1764 to around 1780.[16] Christoph von Jünger was given protection to produce enamels (presumably free of being implicated under the terms of the monopoly of the Imperial Porcelain Factory). He did not limit himself to boxes and trinkets, but also produced domestic vessels of considerable size, in imitation of Sèvres porcelain popular at that time. Christoph von Jünger died in 1777, but his brother Johann continued the factory until his death in 1780. The small cup and tray shown were thought to be of Staffordshire origin when acquired by the Victoria and Albert Museum in 1868. The cup is unusually small and there is a possibility that the von Jünger workshops made objects mainly for the Oriental market.

Ornamentation of enamel boxes in England changed course in the late 1760s. As early as 1759 in France, in philosophical circles, D'Alembert wrote 'a most remarkable change in our ideas is taking place'. He was describing the winds of change which were blowing through the *salons*, 'sweeping out the Rococo curves and all the posturing Commedia dell'Arte figures and other exquisite frivolities and perversities which had delighted a fastidious, over-sophisticated society'.[17] Rococo in this form had not really been seen in England, and in the field of enamels only in a very anglicised way. The bordering of the box was inevitably the most rococo element. However, in 1759 Decker published *Gothic Architecture* showing a large collection of temples, gazebos, alcoves, obelisks, pyramids, '. . . many of which may be executed with Pollards, Rude Branches, and roots of trees, being a taste entirely new'. Seven years later in England Robert Mainwaring published *The Cabinet and Chair-makers real friend and companion.* This, combined with the publication of the finds from the excavations in Herculaneum and Pompeii (published in 1757) and also

[16] Charleston, R., 'Christoph and Johann von Jünger, enamel manufacturers in Vienna', *Antiques*, 1959, p. 334.

[17] Honour, op. cit., p. 17.

An Austrian cup and saucer enamelled on copper by Christoph von Jünger.
Vienna, *c.* 1765.
Cup: 2¼ in. high.
Victoria and Albert Museum

A Bilston snuff-box painted with a portrait of Miss Nancy Dawson, the celebrated actress and dancer, who appeared at Sadlers Wells and Covent Garden. Her career ended in 1767.
c. 1765.
3 in. wide.

Sotheby & Co.

Piranesi's views of Rome plus the growing liking of the English for the Grand Tour, made itself felt in the painting of boxes. The scenes from the *Ladies Amusement* which had provided inspiration for the previous generation were now replaced by views of decaying ruins set in an ideal English park. But the rococo scroll border survived until hardcore neo-classicism set in in the 1780s.

The severe lines of Adam and the stern choice of materials and colours manifest in Wedgwood's products edged Staffordshire into decline.

A Staffordshire snuff-box with a gallant and his lady seated in a chair of exaggerated rococo form.
Possibly Wednesbury, *c.* 1767.
3⅛ in. diameter.

Sotheby & Co.

Above
A navette-shaped snuff-box in Staffordshire style, probably by Samson of Paris.
c. 1700.
4¼ in. long.

Sotheby & Co.

Below
A Staffordshire enamel beaker, flanked by two mustard pots, the ground colours following the fashionable Sèvres colours.
c. 1755.
Beaker, 2¾ in. high. Pots, about 4½ in. high.
Sotheby & Co.

Their brightly coloured boxes, so popular for thirty years, had to give way to a palette of Etruscan brown and black.

One of the last groups of full-size snuff-boxes, some of which were for use as patch-boxes, reflected the importance of the cotton industry in Lancashire. These are mostly decorated with raised flowers against a 'cotton' background. After 1790, until the end of the Napoleonic War, Birmingham supplied England and parts of Europe with an endless stream of patch-boxes. During the earlier wartime period some of these were painted as *memento mori*, with a mourning figure leaning over a classical altar. In this can be seen the neo-classical concept of death, 'the emphasis being shifted from the problematical joys of the blessed in Paradise to the more tangible love, admiration and grief of the survivors on earth. The hero takes the place of the saint in the iconography of death.'[18] The final type is the true souvenir box, either for bon-bons or for patches; these are usually inscribed with the name of the town in which they were sold to the visitor. The legend often starts with 'A trifle from . . .' . The later the boxes, the more vivid in colour the base.

During the Regency period the style of men's coats changed and the snuff-box had to be considerably reduced in size to conform to the new slender silhouette. This really effectively swept the surviving types of enamel boxes, of which there were very few, out of fashion. Silver and gold snuff-boxes were made to fit the pocket and were extremely shallow; enamel on copper, incorporating the two thicknesses, would have been totally impractical. New types of boxes, such as those of pressed wood and horn and those in papier mâché, became popular.

For almost half-a-century the enamels of South Staffordshire had been much in demand. They had been of sufficiently good quality to attract the wealthiest of patrons and it is significant that the extravagant gold and enamel box was never as popular in England as it was in France. The reason for this is found in the social structure of England during the second half of the 18th century. The aristocracy of the period included not only the great nobles but the squires, the wealthier clergy, and the cultivated middle-class. In Boswell's Johnsonian dialogues,[19] and in the life histories of the most professional men, that great society, broad-based on adequate numbers, and undisputed in its social privilege, could afford to look for quality in everything – the leaders of the 18th century were not harassed by the perpetual itch to make money and yet more money, to produce more and yet more goods no matter of what sort, as were those mighty children of mammon who in the 19th century set the tone for England, America and all the world. The aristocratic atmosphere was more favourable to art and taste than either the bourgeois or democratic have since proved to be in England, or the totalitarian in Europe. Indeed, aristocracy functioned better as a patron of art and letters than even the old-fashioned form of kingship. The English aristocracy had not one centre but hundreds scattered all over the country in 'gentlemen's seats' and provincial towns, each of them a focus of learning and taste that more than made up for the decay of learning at the official universities and of taste at the Hanoverian court.

This was the social context in which the enamel producers, together with an export business on the Continent, found a market. However, the vogue for painted enamels more or less expired before the end of the Napoleonic Wars and wasn't revived – and even then in a totally different form – until almost a century later.

Battersea and Staffordshire enamels began to be collected at the end of the last century and it was then that the first of the copies appeared. The exact number of workshops producing these is not known, but many of the copies of full-size snuff-boxes made around 1900 bear the interlaced S mark of the factory of Emil Samson of Paris which specialised in copying 18th century porcelain and enamels. Over the passage of time, many of the signatures have been erased but there are several known types which differ from the originals and that were obviously produced in quantity.

[18] ibid., pp. 146–58.

[19] Trevelyan, G. M., *Illustrated English Social History*, vol. 3, p. 191.

A snuff-box, probably by Samson of Paris, imitating the Staffordshire originals of around 1765.
About 3½ in. wide.

Sotheby & Co.

The snuff-box illustrated is somewhat larger than was the Staffordshire original and apart from the obvious difference in the actual process of enamelling which is evident in the 'depth' of the enamel, created by a thick impasto of translucent enamel, the mounts are somewhat inferior. This last point is immediately recognisable in many of the copies; the Staffordshire hinges and mounts were usually of good quality and function extremely efficiently today, yet the copyists working only half-a-century ago used a thinner gauge of metal for their productions and by doing so made a short-lived hinge. Consequently the lids sometimes don't close. The other box, of navette shape, shows a conflict in periods, between the shape popular in boxes post-1785 and the decoration, which is derived from an earlier period. The way in which the rim of the box cuts across a panel of painted decoration suggests that the maker had little knowledge of the original.

Other popular types copied during this century include numerous Trafalgar relics; patch-boxes decorated with a portrait of Nelson or of a sea battle; or alternatively 'cock-fighting' boxes which usually have brightly coloured bases. The more unusual English enamels, invariably in relief-work, were thought to be too difficult to copy. Samson's copies weren't necessarily made to deceive, but after fifty years they have a worn surface that the modern collector might find convincing.

Right
A Jamaican incised tortoise-shell comb, in case.
Late 17th century.
4 in. long.

Sotheby & Co.

Cheaper Substitutes

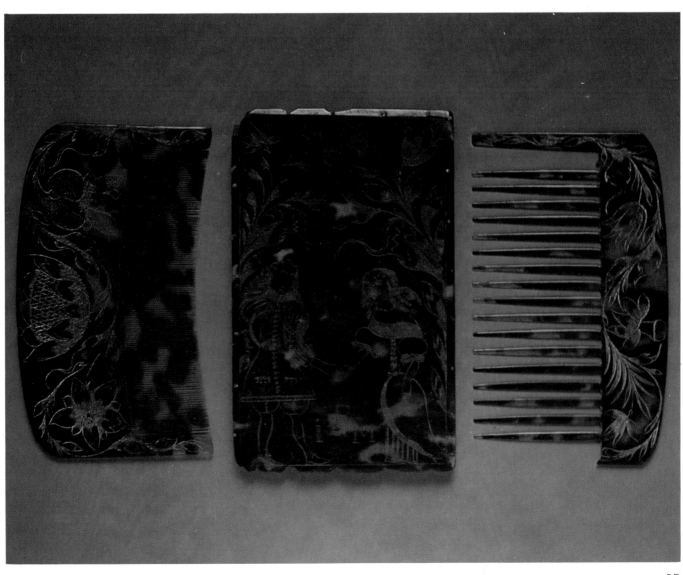

An ivory snuff rasp, the reverse with a steel
grater and snuff compartment.
Dieppe, c. 1690–1700.
7¾ in.

Private collection

Above
A fruitwood casket for jewels or papers by
Bagart of Nancy.
Late 17th century.
12 in. wide.

Sotheby & Co.

Right
Apparently the only recorded snuff-box
with an Obrisset plaque of Charles II. The
box also by Obrisset, mounted in gold.
London, *c.* 1705.
3⅜ in. long.

Private collection

The Drake Box, in pressed horn, by John
Obrisset, dated 1712.
4 in. wide.

Park Antiques

A tortoise-shell *piqué* box with the Fox and
Stork from Æsop's Fables.
c. 1725.
2½ in. wide.

M. Hakim

Most snuff-boxes surviving from the 17th century, when not made of gold or silver, are inevitably in horn or tortoise-shell, which was also used for the manufacture of other objects such as pounce-pots and tobacco boxes. These snuff-boxes were made in great quantities both in England and on the Continent and their popularity was only to wane with the emergence of brightly lacquered wares in the late 18th century.

Tortoise-shell was known to the English in the mid-17th century when Jamaican tortoise-shell combs began to arrive in this country. They were usually contained in a flat case decorated with an incised design. By the end of the 17th century the shell itself was being imported from Asia where it was obtained from the Hawksbill turtle. Since the Dutch had close links with the East at that time they were probably the principal carriers. Horn on the other hand was obtainable in Europe until demand for lanterns was so great at the end of the 17th century that it had to be imported from America.[1]

Both of these materials were malleable, which allowed for decoration in precious metals when softened; there were three alternatives: the material could be worked either by pressing or tooling or by inlaying in gold or silver. The horn or tortoise-shell could be softened by boiling in water with a drop of olive oil, or else by dipping it in mustard.

One of the first craftsmen to exploit the malleability of both media was John Obrisset, the son of a Huguenot ivory carver from Dieppe who came to England presumably about the time of the Revocation of the Edict of Nantes (1685). His technique of pressing horn and tortoise-shell was probably learnt from working on ivory in Dieppe, the centre of the ivory trade in Europe in the 17th century. He settled in London and as far as we know started making horn boxes moulded with portrait heads, after medallions, around 1690. Obrisset was still working in 1712, but after that nothing is recorded. By the second quarter of the 18th century pressed horn played a less prominent part and was not revived on a viably commercial footing until the end of the century.

Tortoise-shell, on the other hand, had a more lasting success. This is probably because it provided an attractive dark background colour

[1] le Corbeille, op. cit., p. 83.

Above
A Regency *boîte à mouches*, with piqué hairwork decoration, by Jean Fouquet.
Paris, 1726.
2⅛ in. wide.

Sotheby & Co.

against which silver or gold decoration showed to good advantage. From 1690 onwards tortoise-shell *piqué* boxes were to be produced in numerous countries, mainly Holland, England and France, and later in Germany and Italy, in great quantities. As very few of these boxes are signed or inscribed in any way it is somewhat difficult to sort out the various regions of manufacture with any degree of accuracy. However, the first group of bun-shaped boxes, which are opened by squeezing both ends at the same time to release the spring lid, were often decorated with large *clous*; this type is certainly English. Slightly later, around 1720, this decoration was refined to the *piqué point* technique in which different coloured gold pin-head dots were inlaid. At the same time the more effective technique of hairwork came into being in which thin strips of gold or silver were let into the shell. This developed into *piqué posé* which was the most attractive of all, and is the technique of inlaying sheet metal.

The fables of La Fontaine were executed in both techniques. The large fat bun-shaped box is French and is quite often made of 'blond tortoise-shell'. These *boîtes à ballons* are perhaps the most attractive of all tortoise-shell objects. They were popular in France around the middle of the 18th century and were probably used for bon-bons or dragees.

Naples was also an important centre for tortoise-shell and from her workshops came an assortment of objects including games boxes, ink stands and large caskets, as well as snuff-boxes. An example of the latter, decorated with a view of Vesuvius, must date from the 1760s. The success of the Naples factories was assured when the city became an important stopping-off point on the Grand Tour.

An oval snuff-box decorated in gold *piqué posé*, with a view of the Bay of Naples, and a *boîte à ballons* with *piqué point* and *posé* decoration.
Italian, third quarter of 18th century.
$2\frac{7}{8}$ and $2\frac{3}{4}$ in. wide.
Private collection

Around the middle of the century engine-turning was first applied as a decorative feature in box-making. By the mid-1760s the factory of Boulton and Fothergill was producing them in quantities; from this moment on industrialisation of the cheaper type of box set in and after this the most prolifically produced boxes, with the exception of lacquered boxes, were those in horn and wood pressed with varying types of ornament.

France had led European fashion for the whole of the 18th century and as the political climate changed and it was thought more judicious to carry a simple box, so tortoise-shell came back into popularity again. Yet by 1780 tortoise-shell was well into decline. It did not conform to the neo-classical colour scheme and pressed wood and lacquered papier mâché took over from it.

Wood boxes

Boxes and small trinkets fashioned out of wood were common in the 17th century. These were naturally of varying quality; the great majority of those surviving today were produced provincially for a local market and do not attempt to be more than what they are. Anyone wanting a snuff container could buy one in wood, either plainly carved or with simple decoration.

However, there are two main types of wood boxes which were professionally marketed. The first is the school of fruitwood carvers producing 'form' boxes at the end of the 17th and beginning of the 18th centuries, probably in the Low Countries. Some of the most attractive of their pieces are those of boat form – a particularly popular theme in the northern European countries – and which was to be reproduced in all materials. The hulls were carved with finely detailed work, and even the cherubs on the poop are worked. Another type is the flattened bun-shaped box carved with portrait heads within strapwork and scrolls.

In France the most prolific workshops were those of Bagard of Nancy. His workshops, using fruitwood, turned out an assortment of boxes of varying sizes, a few for snuff, but the majority, ranging from about 8 inches to 14 inches in width, for various other uses. His craftsmen worked in very low relief, quite often incorporating the arms of the owner within more conventional decoration.

The second, and most prolific group, are those which were pressed with a variety of decorations. These are first mentioned around 1770, but it wasn't until the beginning of the next decade that they were appearing in great numbers. Part of their initial success must have been due to their appeal to a society at that moment attracted by the neo-classical craze for cameo collecting; nearly all these boxes were of circular form, unhinged and rather shallow. The lids were moulded with classical scenes or simply with portrait heads, the bases occasionally with engine-turned decoration, but usually remaining absolutely plain. At a later stage the sides were cut in a concave shape to facilitate the opening and shutting of the box; it had been found that if a residue of snuff was lodged between the lip and the cover it was very difficult to remove the lid. They were very rarely fitted with metal rim mounts.

Many of the chief producers of these boxes were in France and during the 1790s and Empire period the subject matter was chosen more to educate the user than to please his eye. Rather like the Frederick the Great commemorative boxes they were used as a vehicle for propaganda. Most of the subjects were topical and referred to contemporary events; portraits of Louis XVI appeared before the Revolution, and those of Louis XVIII, Charles X and Louis Philippe afterwards, but their portraits are all too rare compared with the incredible output of circular maple boxes pressed with the portrait and military successes of the Emperor Napoleon.

A spate of Napoleonic boxes commemorated his death in 1821, and by far the largest proportion of pressed maple boxes that survive today are of this type – those decorated with Bacchic and other scenes are rare and were probably done after the restoration of the monarchy. The ultimate in education is to be found on a box in which the theories of Dr Joseph Gall have been expounded. He had given a series of lectures on human craniology in Paris in the spring of 1808 and as fashion didn't want to lag behind and not honour the good Doctor, the *Tabatière Cranéologique* was produced so that 'our men of fashion' were familiar with the marvels that the Doctor had propounded and by taking a pinch of tobacco (snuff) could achieve a complete course in craniology.[2]

Lacquered and Varnished Boxes

The Dutch East India Company first imported Japanese screens into Europe in the 17th century. They were immediately popular, but the Japanese government then placed an embargo on their export; demand outstripped supply, and so the copyists moved in to alleviate this position.

Between 1670 and 1690 several treatises were published on the technique of 'Japanning' as it was then called. At that time it was assumed that the varnish was applied to a wood ground but during the following century it had a more general meaning and the base material could also be metal or papier mâché.

[2] D'Allemagne, op. cit., p. 137.

Below
A Neapolitan tortoise-shell ink-stand decorated in gold *piqué posé* and mother-of-pearl. The arms are those of the Medici. Mid-18th century.
10½ in. high.

M. Hakim

Right
A dressing table box of japanned tinned iron sheet set with a Staffordshire plaque. The plaque is enamelled with a classical scene which includes the Colosseum, a torso and an equestrian statue of Marcus Aurelius.
Midlands or possibly London, *c.* 1755.
10¼ in. long, 7¼ in. wide.

M. Hakim

The first successful commercial application of lacquering, around 1725, was at Pontypool in South Wales. Major John Hanbury turned part of his family iron works over to the production of snuff-boxes and other objects with a thin iron body, tinned and painted with chinoiseries. This was in the 1740s. The factory remained in existence until 1822, but there is no doubt that their later output consisted mainly of trays, urns and tea caddies. Their snuff-boxes could never compete with those of a fairly cheap type of painted enamel from the Staffordshire workshops after *c*. 1760. One of the disadvantages was that they were not as durable as enamelled copper boxes, and they were susceptible to peeling and chipping which exposed the base metal and made them look very dowdy.

In the late 1730s the process of japanning was taken up in Birmingham by John Taylor (1711–*c*. 1775) and by John Baskerville. They imitated the Pontypool method until the middle of the century, but then Taylor, who was already producing painted enamels, gave up metal as a base material, and instead employed papier mâché which proved lighter and more durable than its predecessor.[3]

[3] William Hutton, writing of John Taylor in 1781, recorded that 'one servant earned three pounds ten shillings per week by painting snuff-boxes at a farthing each'. This must have referred to the application of a monochrome coat, since it is unlikely that any workman, even in an 80 hour week, could paint over 40 boxes an hour with anything more than a simple device.

A circular lacquered box, signed *Stobwasser's Fabrik in Braunschweig*, and painted with an amusing scene of billeted soldiers, with the legend inscribed, *pousée donc coquin! j'écoute, j'écoute*, and with the stock number *8932*
Early 19th century.
3¾ in. diameter.

Park Antiques

In England there was always a demand for lacquered boxes; the painters copied fashionable engravings of the day and political and satirical boxes were common during the Napoleonic wars. After 1815 coloured or monochrome circular engravings were glued on the body of the box and fixed with a thick coat of varnish. Many of these engravings were either French or German or even American, made for export.

Stobwasser

The only real competition that the Birmingham makers had on the Continent were the products of the Stobwasser family in Brunswick. Stobwasser boxes were for the most part identical with the English counterparts – circular, a little over 3½ inches in diameter, with black sides, base and interior, the lids brilliantly painted and the subjects usually identified inside the lid, in red, together with the signature of the factory. The firm had been founded by Georg Siegmund Stobwasser, who was given leave by Karl I of Brunswick to settle there, and had been granted a monopoly of the production of japanned trays, boxes and even furniture, in 1769.

Vernis Martin

In France undoubtedly the most important name in varnished wares was that of Guillaume Martin who was made *vernisseur du roi*, an honour which devolved after his death in 1749 on his two brothers Etienne Simon and Robert. They had three factories in action in Paris during the 1750s and 1760s when *vernis Martin* was really at its height of fashion. They produced furniture – their *bureau de dames* being especially popular – snuff- and powder-boxes, bodkin cases and other small objects. Their decoration

The lid of a Louis XV *vernis martin* powder box showing the unusual *piqué posé* decoration on the border.
Paris, 1761.
3⅜ in. diameter.

M. Hakim

did not in any way pretend to be Japanese, instead the inspiration for their ornament stemmed from paintings by Boucher and other contemporary favourites.

Most boxes and cases that are to be found today are painted with *fêtes champêtres* or simply with plump Bacchic putti shown against either green or golden grounds. Their colours certainly did not conform to the neo-classical preference for attic tones of terracotta and black and this is probably why little is heard of the Martin brothers' work after the 1780s. By then Birmingham and the Stobwasser factories were in the ascendancy and were to remain supreme until 1830 when, like snuff itself, the box went out of fashion.

The Early 19th Century

The Later Snuff-box in France and England

It was not until about thirteen years after the Revolution that a change in the political and social climate in France allowed for the return of accessories made of precious metals. Things had been so bad for the luxury trades in 1797 that the Marquis d'Avèze, the commissioner of the factories of Sèvres, Savonnerie and the Gobelins, had arranged a bazaar for the sale of craftsmen's work. This was the first major French National Exhibition and proved such a success that it was repeated the next year. It was

An Empire presentation box by Adrien M. Vachette, the lid with a miniature of the Empress Josephine.
Early 19th century.
3¾ in. wide.

Sotheby & Co.

Right
Scent bottle, enamelled in *basse taille* technique.
c. 1830.
4 in. (suspended).

Sotheby & Co.

only in this way that the craftsmen producing luxury objects could find a market. Fortunately Napoleon himself was a snuff-taker and fully understood the significance and use of a rich-looking diplomatic gift. His *orfèvre bijoutier* was Adrien-Joseph-Maximilien Vachette who was received master in 1779 and died in 1839. His work was of a particularly high standard when compared with Swiss boxes of the same period and was certainly close to the quality achieved by the English box-makers, who at this period were working almost exclusively in gold. His boxes were of shallow oblong form, heavy and with beautifully constructed hinges.

Some were fairly modest in appearance, with enamel miniatures by or after Petitot set into tortoise-shell with gold linings. In the more extravagant boxes the engine-turned panels were bordered by boldly-cut leaves and enclosed either cameos or portrait miniatures. Such a box bearing a portrait miniature of the Empress Josephine by Jean-Baptiste Isabey and made by Vachette as a presentation box from Josephine to M. le Comte de Béarn is decorated with a plain border in blue enamel – Prussian blue having only been developed in 1810.[1] It is also interesting to see the

[1] Evans, op. cit., p. 124.

Snuff-box by Gabriel-Raoul Morel, chased in four-colour gold and with a background of sepia-coloured mother-of-pearl. Paris, 1819–38.
$3\frac{1}{4}$ in. wide.

Private collection

An Austrian presentation snuff-box, given by His Imperial Highness, The Archduke Frederick of Austria, to Captain Milne, September 1842.
$3\frac{1}{4}$ in. wide.

Sotheby & Co.

[2] The guild system, which had been in operation since mediæval times, allowed for the existence of the highly specialist craftsman. Consequently a very high standard was maintained. After the dissolution of the guild system there is no doubt that the standard of craftsmanship in France went into gradual decline, steeply so after the retirement of such men as Vachette, who had been apprenticed and received master under the old system.

retailer's name appearing in full on the lid of the box. During the previous century only a few names appeared, and all too rarely. However, this change might have been brought about by the termination of the goldsmiths' guild, *c.* 1790.[2]

French box making after the restoration of the monarchy is best embodied in the works of Gabrielle Raoul Morel who continued in the old styles of the *Ancien Régime* yet never seemed to stay long with the same technique. In another maker's work the rather Germanic type of *basse-taille* enamelling, which was in use there in the 17th century, appears on a scent-bottle (dating from the mid-1830s) made to be suspended from a ring worn over a glove. This, together with a more elaborate form of scent-bottle enamelled in the mid-18th century manner, shows the beginnings of revivalism in the field of the arts in the second quarter of the 19th century. Snuff-taking was in decline; there was little demand for elaborate boxes – no longer did snuff-takers have collections of boxes of high quality. This had of course begun after the Revolution when the French luxury industries collapsed and the Swiss workshops, mainly in Geneva, took the initiative.

Scent flaçon of serpentine, the gold cage-work with enamelled flowers.
Possibly English or Dutch, *c.* 1835.
2 9/16 in. long.
Wartski, London

The Swiss enamelling industry had, until 1790, concentrated on the decoration of watches. Until that time comparatively few boxes were made and these were mostly in imitation of Paris designs, sometimes even struck with spurious French marks. But their particular forte was enamelling, and by 1800 the workshops of Geneva were selling boxes abroad, the lids set with miniatures, which did not chip or scratch badly because they were now coated with a thick protective layer of transparent enamel which was fired over the finished painting. This meant that miniatures painted in enamel could be done on a larger scale now that the risk of potential damage was diminished and so the French style of oblong box was chosen as a suitable shape to display to the full the qualities of Swiss enamelling.

From 1800 to 1850 Swiss boxes were shallow, oblong and with rounded corners, and the base panels were countersunk. The decoration was in enamel, perhaps with engine-turning beneath; occasionally these boxes are marked but as yet few makers have been identified. However, the goldsmiths must have taken second place to the enamellers. It is known that there were as many as 77 enamel painters in Geneva in 1789, but unfortunately few of these have been identified as yet. Nevertheless, one enameller fortunately signed some of his work: this was Jean-Louis Richter (1766–1841) who, like his mentors, the Roux brothers, specialised in landscapes.

The other type of subject that proved most popular was entirely neo-classical in inspiration. Under the Empire the idea of art as education was transformed into that of art as propaganda and centred on the cult of the Emperor. No longer did the mythological beauties of an earlier period charm the viewer; the status of the female was debased. In Roman times man had power of life or death over his wife. This philosophy emerged in the paintings of the lids and follows the works of the most fashionable painters of the day.

The designers in Geneva adapted the most heroic scenes and obviously took Reynold's comments to heart. Speaking of painters' choice of subject matter he declared that none 'can be proper that is not generally interesting. It ought to be either some instance of heroick action or heroick suffering. There must be something either in the action or in the subject in which men are universally concerned and which powerfully strikes upon the publick sympathy.'[3]

[3] As quoted by Honour, op. cit., p. 42.

A Swiss enamelled musical snuff-box with a neo-classical scene.
1810–20.
3¼ in. wide.

M. Hakim

A Swiss enamelled gold snuff-box, the lid
decorated with Pan and Syrinx.
Geneva, *c.* 1790.
3 in. wide.

Sotheby & Co.

The interior of a base panel on a Swiss box
painted in the manner of Richter with
lakeside scenes.
Early 19th century.
2¾ in. diameter.

M. Hakim

Many of these scenes were taken from the works of Greuse, David, Nicholas-Guy Brenet, and Jean-Baptiste Régnault. Many of these subjects are really not in sympathy with modern taste but during this high-water mark of neo-classicism the 'power of a work of art to touch the heart, as well as to instruct and be morally improving' was easily accepted by those who agreed with Lessing that the 'most compassionate man is the best man . . . and he who makes us compassionate makes us better and more virtuous'.

Geneva produced what the export markets required. Their box trade was important but not as important as their 'automata' trade – an extension of their specialist horological knowledge. They were to be the best known makers of automata and musical objects for at least a century: their inventions were to be imitated but never equalled in this luxury field. There are three main sub-divisions which fall under this general heading.

The first is the singing bird box, a speciality of the firm of Jacquet-Droz. From their experience in producing automata figures on clocks for the Spanish Royal Family in the 1750s, they began working on a fully automated singing bird. From the moment Henri-Louis Jacquet-Droz's (1752–1791) first singing bird box appeared it established this type of automata as perhaps the most popular of all. The boxes were of conventional shape, with an oval cover set in the centre of the lid, which, at the touch of a button, flipped up and out popped a feathered bird with flapping wings, head moving from side to side and singing a song. When the mechanism unwound the bird disappeared and the lid snapped shut. These were much in demand at the beginning of the 19th century and were exported in varying qualities. The most expensive type was of gold and enamel, and

An extremely rare Swiss double singing bird box, signed *Rochat frères*. $4\frac{1}{8}$ in. long.

M. Hakim

one of the rarest types was a double singing bird box. The success of this model stimulated Jacquet-Droz to produce an occasional scent-pistol or flacon. Later in the century came the singing bird box in tortoise-shell – the finer examples with enamelled bird covers were sold in red morocco cases complete with keys. Later in the century they were to be entirely industrialised, the cases made of alloy cast with 18th-century-style ornament. Jacquet-Droz had opened an agency in London in 1785 but this was probably principally as an outlet for watches. Nine years later Horace Walpole wrote to Mary Berry: 'A Parisian watch maker (has) produced the smallest automaton that I suppose was ever created. It was a rich snuff-box, not too large for a woman. On opening the lid, an enamelled bird started up, sat on the rim, turned round, fluttered its wings, and piped in a delightful tone the notes of different birds; particularly the jug-jug of the nightingale – only five hundred pounds. That economist, the Prince of Wales, could not resist it, and has bought one of those dicky-birds.'

Walpole assumed that this was a French invention although it was almost certainly a bird box from the Jacquet-Droz and Leschot factory. Although many bear the firm's hallmark, few of their boxes were actually signed in full,[4] and because of this retailer-jewellers and goldsmiths in any centre could claim their stock as pure London or Paris work which commanded a higher price. Another specialist was Jacob Frisard (1753–1812), who had worked for Jacquet-Droz in London and Geneva.

The second series were the various types of musical box which was a German speciality. The movements were of pin-barrel and comb type, and were set beneath a horn cover, above which was allowed a small space for snuff.

These were in commercial production after about 1810 – although a few are known before this date – one of the earliest plays an original setting of the Marseillaise. Some of the earliest are thought to have been exported as movements; some certainly appear in French tortoise-shell and pressed horn cases. The finer quality boxes, using a combination of dark blue enamel and engine-turned gold in the manner of Vachette appeared a little later. Two miniature harps with musical movements in the base are fitted with suspension chains but were surely impractical as 'fobs'. The maker whose work is associated with musical movements above all others is Isaac-David Piquet (1775–1841).

The third series of objects comprises automata. As with the musical and singing bird boxes, the automata figures which appeared in Swiss objects of vertu were transplanted by them from an earlier horological setting. Animated scenes were very popular from 1815 onwards, usually in conjunction with musical movements, and they were included in objects varying from standing scent-bottles, watches and boxes down to sealing-wax cases, rings and fob seals. The more expensive the object, the more intricate the automata. One of the most admired is the magician box

[4] Some of the more complicated automata boxes are signed in full, but the signatures are lost from sight behind the intricate components.

Right
A Swiss snuff-box in the form of a sheep.
Early 19th century.
2¼ in. long.

M. Hakim

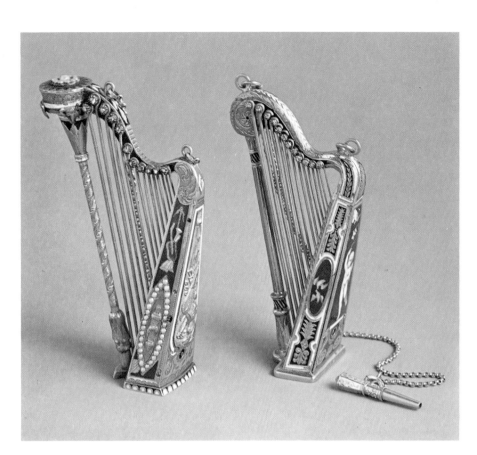

Two Swiss musical harps.
Early 19th century.
About 2 in. high.

M. Hakim

A standing scent bottle with automata scene and musical accompaniment of a carillon of six bells.
Geneva, early 19th century.
8⅛ in. high.

M. Hakim

perfected by Frères Rochat (active during the first quarter of the 19th century). In another, a group of musicians play to a harpsichord accompaniament and at the end of the recital the seated beau applauds.

Neo-classicism was an intellectual art – it had started off as a vision of 'a pure noble and uncorrupt world', but by now it had undergone change during a prolonged war and was being industrialised. By 1820 there was very little of the licentiousness of Louis XV snuff-boxes painted with figures of Venus and Bacchantes to be found in decorations or ornament. Instead of the earlier quasi-eroticism the Swiss makers offered a fully automated form of erotica – hidden from view and incorporated in a watch or seal. Double-lidded boxes and boxes with secret sliding lids had been fairly common in the past, but a fully animated musically accompanied scene proved even more popular. Both watch and fob were easily portable and the mechanical detail and perfection of the hidden scene would certainly prove to be an entertainment for the owner's friends.

The Swiss never lost their supremacy in the field of mechanical toys and objects. This, together with its watch industry, contributed to the country's economic growth and their position in this luxury market is very strong even today. The enamelling workshops in Geneva continued through the decline of this industry in the rest of Europe, which occurred from 1810 until 1850, and were even producing fine enamelled watchbacks in the 1920s.

A 'manual automatum' in which the dining table disappears into the floor to reveal a *scène grivois* at present hidden from view. The device is operated by revolving the bezel.
Early 19th century.
3 in.

Sotheby & Co.

England. Regency and later

England during the Regency period was very fashion conscious. Endless
satirical drawings survive which poked fun at every innovation. Yet there
were serious fashion plates published at this time, year by year, and in
them one can see the rise and fall of each fashion. Quizzing glasses for
ladies came in around 1814 and stayed in fashion until around 1830 when
they lost status. They were usually very simple, with a lens in a gold frame
and a loop for a silk ribbon. After this date the construction was more
elaborate and they eventually evolved later in the century into the
lorgnette for the lady and the monocle for the gentleman. The spy-glass
is also shown in fashion plates; the young girl uses one to scan the English
Channel during the Napoleonic Wars; these gradually evolved into
binoculars and opera glasses in the middle of the century.

Fob seals also came into their own during this period; previously they

Two Regency quizzing glasses flanking a lorgnette with single lens.
Early 19th century.
3 and 5½ in. long.

M. Hakim

had only been one of the many fittings on the chatelaine, but now the chatelaine was simplified so that all attention was fixed on the seal. The quality varied enormously and quite often the lower quality ones were made of low carat gold. It is possible to date them by the shape of the superstructure. The early ones are in Adam style with the intaglio open on both sides, whilst in the early 19th century the intaglio was enclosed by a cover at the back which is often gadrooned. It wasn't until 1815 to 1820 that the superstructure got heavier and elaborately fashioned with stylised flowers in multi-coloured gold. One of the most delightful series of seals, carved in hardstone with blackamoor heads, might well have been Italian or German, and probably date from the last decade of the 18th century.

In the 1830s the mediæval revival brought about a change in form and styles generally. The success of the Waverley novels in England and the publicity surrounding the Eglintoun Tournament in 1837 combined to reproduce a 'gothick' atmosphere and a society conscious of knightly lineage and heraldry. By this time men's costume had changed and as breeches gave way to fuller trousers so the wearing of fobs declined. Instead, the desk seal or hand seal, with a hardstone or heavily ornamented handle came in. Owing to the convenience of having both one's family

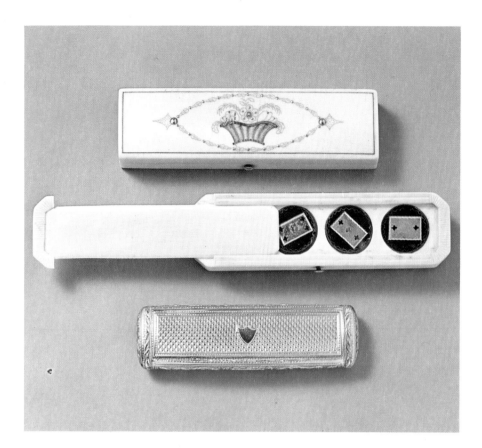

Two English ivory toothpick cases, one with a concealed aperature for flat dice, and a Swiss engine-turned gold case.
Swiss, early 19th century.
3 in., 3¾ in., 2½ in. long.

Private collection

English romantic snuff-box, with miniatures of Charlotte and Werthe, inspired by Goethe's poem written in 1772, and later translated into English as 'The Sorrows of Young Werther'.
Early 19th century.
2¾ in. diameter.

Sotheby & Co.

arms and crest on the same seal, the swivel seal was given a handle and the multi-sided seal was mounted to facilitate rotation. A return to courtly ideals as revived at Eglintoun probably influenced the gauntletted-arm seals, complete in all details from the upper and lower canons to the counter. The truncation at the shoulder was used for one seal whilst the baton served to accommodate a further two.

Victor Hugo, whose novels had really sparked off the gothic revival in France, in 1841 addressed two lines of poetry to Francois-Désiré Froment-

Meurice (1802–55), the celebrated jeweller:

'Le poète est ciseleur,
Le ciseleur est poète.'

This inspired him to produce a few bracelets in pure gothic style with scenes from the life of St Louis, followed two years later by others entitled 'Esmerelda' and 'Jeanne d'Arc', but as public support was lacking, and as the Academy in 1846 was protesting against the building of churches in gothic style, Froment-Meurice turned his attention to the Renaissance for inspiration.

He took to the decoration of book covers and one of the most elaborate examples executed at any period was produced in Paris around the time of the 1848 Revolution. The end papers of this missal are signed by Alphonse Simier, the Royal Bookbinder, and the enamelled silver-gilt cover is, according to Vever, in Romantic Renaissance style,[5] but which would today be more aptly described as late Gothic. Froment-Meurice was the leading jeweller-craftsman of the Romantic period and even

A Scottish snuff mull of a type popular further south in the middle of the 19th century.
c. 1820.
5½ in. high.

M. Hakim

A mediaeval-revival, jewelled, enamelled and silver-gilt book cover, set with an Italian 16th century cameo, by Froment-Meurice of Paris.[5]

c. 1845–50.

$11\frac{7}{8}$ in. (overall length).

Sotheby & Co.

[5]Vever, Henri, *La Bijouterie Française au XIXe Siècle*, H. Floury, Paris, 1906, vol. I, p. 171.

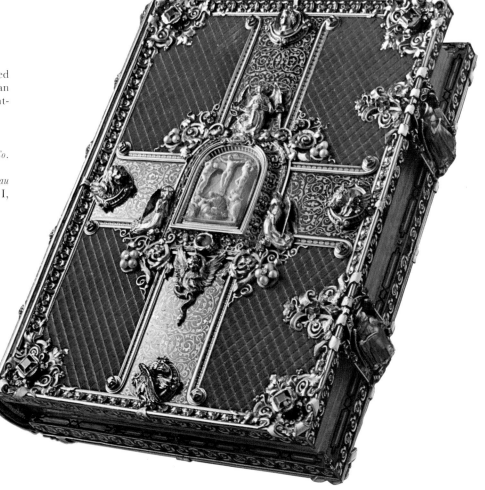

A William IV gold box, chased in high relief with a view of Windsor Castle, by Nathaniel Mills of Birmingham.
1835–6.
3¼ in. wide.

Private collection

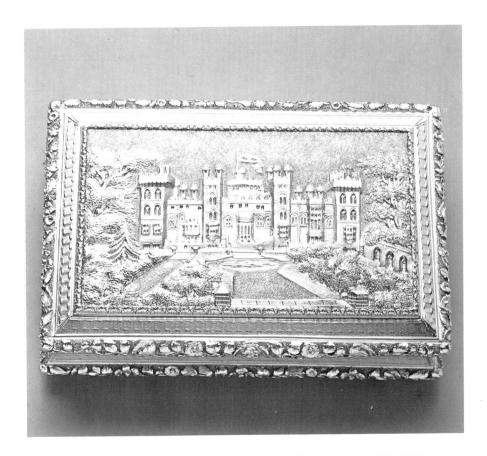

A Charles X 'gothick' snuff-box, decorated in *champlevé* enamel on gold.
Paris, 1824–30.
2⅝ in. wide.

Collection of Lady Jane Rayne

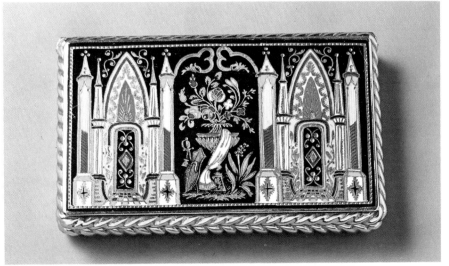

during his most successful spell others were lifting ornament from the previous century, no doubt inspired by the opening of Versailles in 1837 as a national museum.

The gothic revival may have lost ground in France by the mid-19th century, but it had taken a very firm grip on England. This was, however, only the first of a multitude of revivals; it was an eclectic age in which objects of vertu were rendered almost obsolete; in which ornamentation of the house was all-important and in which applied arts were to be industrialised and the best from each country publicly shown and judged at any of the numerous international exhibitions which were to take place.

Exhibition Pieces

'We may not be more moral, more imaginative, nor better educated than
our ancestors, but we have steam, gas, railways, and power looms, while
there are more of us and we have more money to spend.'
　　　　John Hollingshead. *Illustrated Catalogue to the 1862 Exhibition*

The Industrial Revolution had transformed Europe, and England in
particular. The Revolution had brought about a spread of wealth which
reached a broad stratum of society, and in its wake brought the beginnings

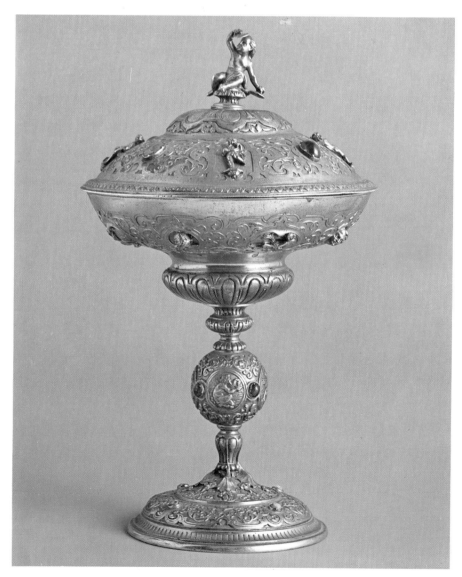

The Cellini Cup, an electro-type by Elkington and Company in Renaissance style.
9¾ in. high.

Private collection

A group of three *zarfs* or Turkish coffee cup holders, made for the Eastern market. Such objects were exhibited in both the 1851 and 1867 Exhibitions.
Swiss or French, mid-19th century.
About 2 in. high.

Sotheby & Co.

of mass production into the applied arts as well as into other fields.

The first International Exhibition of art and industry was held in Hyde Park in 1851. The Great Exhibition was the first of a long stream of international fairs which survive today under the short title of 'Expo'.

Gradually the emphasis has changed over the period of twenty years before the Great Exhibition from a bazaar in which things were for sale alone to an Exhibition where objects were shown to instruct. It had been put on an even more official footing in 1844 when judges were asked to assess the relative qualities of each exhibit and to award gold medals to the most impressive. This action in effect imposed a set of definite standards of aesthetics on both judge and exhibitor which were to remain unaltered for nearly forty years. The artist showing alongside the industrialists' new array of machinery had to conform to the standards set down for the latter. With this imposition of fixed standards, allied with a system of awarding the leaders of each 'class' medals, equating scientific achievement in industry with an artist's achievement, meant that the artist's individual expression was reduced to a modern Olympic-style level – that is, that one must conform to be recognised. This above all protected the revivalist movement in art which was only temporarily laid to rest in the second decade of this century.

Whereas the Industrial Revolution in England had brought about this engagement of industry to art, there was a very good reason why many wanted this alliance to be consummated. Victory at Trafalgar had given England maritime supremacy which was to remain unchallenged until 1916. Maritime trade was in her hands. By 1842 the *Art Union*, one of the first of many art periodicals, and in its way perhaps the most outspoken of all, allowed free discussion in its pages on the association of art and manufacture so as to increase the 'mercantile value of the fine arts'. So, having completely accepted the premise that, with the exception of painting and sculpture, art was only saleable if manufactured, the editorial board went on to investigate the claims industrialists had upon artists and also how best to educate the latter in 'the Arts'. So when in 1849 the 1851 Exhibition was being set up it was proposed to the 'Good Prince Albert' that it should be made international and having had a favourable answer the *Art Union* decided on a propaganda programme to try and clinch it. To publicise the need for an international exhibition and a closer bond between artist and manufacturer they chose and repeated the slogan 'Beauty is cheaper than Deformity'.[1] And so the Great Exhibition opened in this emotionally idealised aesthetic atmosphere.

By the time of the 1851 Exhibition the group of personal objects of

[1] Catalogue of the Paris 1867 Exhibition, *Art Journal*, Virtue & Co, London and New York, 1868, see Introduction.

87

A gold-mounted lapis lazuli tazza in Renaissance style by Charles Duron, exhibited in the Paris Exhibition of 1867. 8¾ in. high.

Private collection

vertu which were essential for the needs of any fashionable person were much reduced. Snuff-taking was in decline, and a sombre choice of colours had entered fashions. The fob seal had given way to the desk seal and the accessories of the previous century were not part of the 19th century social scene. The Exhibition showed original works of art alongside mass-produced works of art; those who wanted to indulge in luxurious objects tended to observe the sober tastes in fashion of the time and instead took to the up-and-coming vogue of ornamenting their drawing rooms at home rather than their persons. The craftsmen who had specialised in gold-smiths work or enamelling or lapidary work now either made jewellery or took to more ambitious schemes. Yet the real exploiter of both public and the craftsman was the industrialist.

One firm helped to maintain England's position in the world markets until 1870. This was Messrs Elkington. They received their first patent in 1840 for electroplating and by 1851 they had perfected their electrotypes which were to prove a great commercial success. Yet much of their success must be attributed to the goldsmiths and designers who were commissioned to produce the prototypes from which the copies were taken. France still held the leading position in Europe for goldsmiths' work and enamelling and it was to her craftsmen that Elkington turned for the prototypes. Elkington's success with cheaply produced electrotypes in the 1850s stimulated the bronze foundry of Barbedienne in Paris to go into competition with a somewhat more substantially produced object. Cast in bronze and decorated with enamel and gilding they proved to be very popular as ornaments in the Victorian room. The revival of interest in mediæval works of art stimulated the return to the technique of *champlevé* enamelling. In this technique the areas of the metal are cut, etched or routed and filled with enamel. This had been a technique used in the Meuse valley workshops during the 12th century, and in the Limoges workshops during the following century, in the production of liturgical works of art. Such a casket by Barbedienne in 12th century style is illustrated.

It was about this time that the ornamentation of the house was becoming fashionable. In 1856 the author of *Elegant Arts for Ladies*, in his essay for the benefit of a newly-wedded girl, states quite categorically that the lady of the house was responsible for the furnishings and that 'a sensible woman will always seek to ornament her house, and to render it attractive, especially as this is the taste of the present day . . .'. By 1876 Barbedienne were producing vases and mantle ornaments for this market. Designs were inspired by Near-Eastern and Algerian imports, all in the *cloisonné* technique of enamelling.

The gothic revival, in decline on the Continent in the 1860s, was punctuated by other revivals. It was a turmoil of periods and styles of decorations. Anything from gothic to Empire could be seen in the fashionable house the year before the Paris Exhibition of 1867. Even then a reaction was setting in against the mixture of styles. In *Le Beau dans l'Utile* (1866) the author complains that there is 'no more style . . . all rooms are alike . . . square boxes; the financiers' taste[2] dominates everything; and luxury takes the place of style . . . every drawing room is a shop full of bric-a-brac, and usually of new bric-a-brac'.

The 1867 Exhibition in Paris however saw two main streams of revived styles – Louis XVI and Renaissance. The first was inspired by the Empress Eugénie who identified herself with Marie Antoinette. The Renaissance, on the other hand, was revived mainly by the new 'art collector'. It was a time of 'Art Treasures' Exhibitions, in which the heirlooms of old families were shown to the public for the first time. As a result possessions became an important element in the minds of the emergent middle classes and the art of the Renaissance goldsmiths was sought after. When the supply dried up the Paris goldsmiths supplied substitutes.

One of the most distinguished was Charles Duron, who unlike his Renaissance counterparts, was able to choose unusually attractive geological specimens of lapis lazuli and other hardstones from mines in Northern Europe which were not being worked in the 16th century. His works are very

[2] The new rich, who were openly emulating existing society and who were creating for themselves an instant 'hereditary' environment by the acquisition of splendid works of art, were sent up in *Punch* (1878) in the different sketches of Sir Gorgius Midas.

distinguished and display an unusually delicate understanding of original techniques and also a fluency of interpretation of the 16th century designs.

The French craftsmen, above all, in the 1867 Paris Exhibition, exhibited works in hardstone and precious metals which were produced in the traditional way. The high standard of craftsmanship remained, yet it was an indication of the wane of the true craftsman that a critic could commend a certain M. Bumeau, who exhibited snuff-boxes, that they were 'very admirably made' and at the same time comment that 'he let us tell the reader that the goldsmiths who can make a really fine snuff-box, perfect in closing and opening from the very lip to the joint, is no mean workman'. Anybody who either collects snuff-boxes or who has examined many examples over the years will fully appreciate the wisdom of this statement. To many today the test of a finely made box is in the hinge. If, after a century or two of constant use the lid closes as if it were operated on a hydraulic system, it is thought to be an unusually fine box. But this was an eclectic age and in the 1860s a few more revived styles came in to join those already popular. Near-Eastern and Algerian objects were in fashion. The art collectors and men of fashion of the day would show old-master drawings and Renaissance works of art against Persian rugs or Moorish hangings. Islamic motifs crept into everything and this mood was exploited by Barbedienne in his Moorish and Eastern-inspired ornaments. Again, the base metal is bronze, enamelled in the *cloisonné* technique. In this, the different colours are divided by wire *cloisons* or barriers. Craftsmen in Europe adopted this technique following the success of Chinese *cloisonné* vases which were being imported in great quantities into Europe. Shortly after this, Elkington in England produced a cheaper version for the 1873 Vienna Exhibition.

By the end of the 1870s the one aim of the interior decorator and designer of furniture was to provide more space to accommodate more and more ornaments. So much so that the French criticised the English furniture designers in the 1878 Exhibition for being influenced too much by '*le goût du bibelot*'.

Science and industry had also transformed the smaller accessories of life which had been so popular in the earlier part of the century. The importance of the 'home life' meant that there was less demand for costly personal accessories. The quality of the ornament in the home was of more importance. Snuff-taking declined after the middle of the century; instead, smoking returned during the Crimean war. It had been thought an undesirable habit for eighty years before this, but in imitation of the English heroes in the trenches before Sevastopol people took up smoking.

The snuff-box also took another knock with the introduction of portrait photography. The Daguerreotype had been the most popular form of portraiture since the 1840s but by the end of the 1860s it was by far the cheapest and most accurate form of portraiture possible. No longer were painters commissioned to paint portrait miniatures for the inside lids of snuff-boxes; their art went into decline, and in America during the Civil War it is interesting to see Daguerreotype cases made to resemble snuff-boxes. A scene of 'The Fortune Teller' cast in relief out of a composition material imitates the technique of pressing wood and horn. (See plates – on p. 93).

The Crimean War had also helped emancipate the position of woman in society. The stories reaching England of Florence Nightingale's initiative encouraged upper and middle class women to take up a professional life and to be of some use to the world. Women were now allowed to walk unaccompanied in public places and to participate in such sports as croquet. The fashion for promenading gave more importance to the parasol handle, which was taken up by the goldsmith and jeweller and given a more feminine line. Fans were still very much a part of a lady's equipment, only to be made redundant by the electric fan at the end of the century. Even the vinaigrette was reduced in size as drainage and sanitation improved; by the 1870s it was so small that elaborate decoration was impractical.

Above right
A casket in bronze, enalled in *champlevé* technique, signed *Barbedienne*, the lid with the monogram of the Emperor Napoleon III. Ferdinand Barbedienne, the founder of the firm, was born in 1810 and died in 1892.
Paris, *c.* 1855.
13½ in. wide.
Private collection

Below right
Covered bowl in gilt bronze with enamelled decoration by Elkington.
London, 1873.
11 in. high.
Two pieces by Barbedienne in *cloisonné* enamel.
c. 1867.
7½ in. high.
Osterreichisches Museum für angewandte Kunst

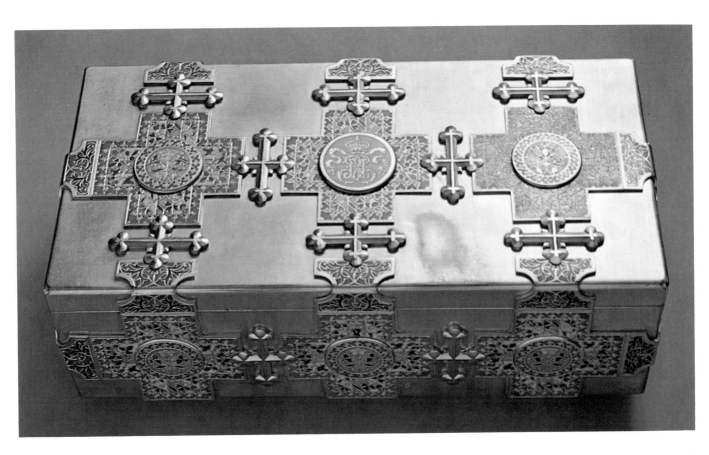

A vesta case and miniature frame by Carlo Giuliano.
c. 1880–90.
Vesta case, 1¾ in. high.

D. Lavender Antiques

Left
Gold-mounted sweetmeat stand in rock crystal by Carlo Giuliano.
c. 1875–80.
4¼ in.

Sotheby & Co.

An American union thermoplastic-daguerreotype case. Inspired by pressed wood snuff boxes, in relief with Gypsy Fortune Teller. Case maker: A. P. Critchlow & Co. *c.* 1857.
5 in.

The emancipated girl of the mid-19th century, discoursing on smoking.

Private collection

Viennese Enamels

From 1773 up to the First World War the most prominent workshops producing enamelled works of art on the Continent, apart from those in Paris and the watch enamellers of Geneva, centred on Vienna. Conforming with the taste of the moment they worked in Renaissance style. Although prolific, the workshops of Vienna hardly ever marked their pieces, and until recently very few, if any, had been identified. Many of the more elaborate examples which display a good level of craftsmanship presumably date from the late 1870s or early 1880s and the occasional piece is marked with the Austro-Hungarian mark for 1866 to 1922. These workshops did a lively export trade and satisfied the needs of the collector who wanted expensive looking Renaissance objects yet who did not mind whether they were of the period or simply 'in the style of' the original.[1]

The firm of Hermann Ratzersdorfer was to specialise in objects for the 19th century collector's *Schatzkammer* from the first exhibition of them in Vienna in 1873 through to the end of the century.[2] Very few if any of the products of his firm were marked. He did not confine his activities to works of art alone, but also merchandised jewellery and made mounts for glass makers. The scope of his firm is shown in the list of objects he exhibited, which included drinking horns, beakers, dishes and caskets. The horn illustrated could still be ordered in 1892[3] and could also be bought in a tooled leather case which was 'aged' to resemble a 16th century original. His stock varied not only in scope but in quality. Comparatively few pieces were mounted in gold – yet the monumental quality and scale of some of the more expensive examples combined with the striking mixtures of materials made them look more grand than the productions of the French goldsmiths in the 1870s.

Vienna was to be the main producer of cheap enamelled and hardstone objects up to the First World War. There are several reasons why this was possible. Although not a particularly prosperous country, Austria emerged in 1866 when the Austro-Hungarian Empire was formed and a dual monarchy was established. This merger gave Austria a ready supply of minerals which were much closer to the capital than was the case in Russia, Vienna's potential competitor in this particular export field. Gold was obtainable in workable quantities both in Bohemia and Transylvania, whilst silver could be obtained in numerous places.

[1] Works of art from private collections were first placed on public view in the 1857 Manchester Art Treasures Exhibition. This above all established art collecting on a broader front.

[2] Feuchtmüller, R., and Mrazek, Dr Wilhelm, *Kunst in Osterreich*, Forum Verlag, Vienna, 1964, p. 95.

[3] Luthmer, F., *Das Email*, E. A. Seemann, Leipzig, 1882, fig. 59.

[4] Palmer, F. H. E., *Austro-Hungarian Life in Town and Country*, Newnes, London, 1903.

[5] One of the finest groups of Milanese 16th century rock crystal objects is in the Schatzkammer der Residenz, Munich.

[6] H. Wieninger was responsible for the wheel cutting on the finer objects from Ratzersdorfer's. In the field of glass the most important firm which specialised in this technique was Lobmeyr. See Rath, S., *Lobmeyr*, Herold, Vienna, 1962, pp. 3 and 4.

Right
A silver mounted wheel-cut crystal horn by Ratzersdorfer.
Vienna, *c.* 1885–90.
26 in. high.

Sotheby & Co.

Over page
Pair of swans in lapis lazuli with enamelled silver heads and feet, and ridden by putti.
Vienna, *c.* 1890.
18 in. high.

Sotheby & Co.

Below
A small box enamelled in the style of the 18th century.
Vienna, 1880–1900.
2 in. diameter.

Sotheby & Co.

Perhaps a key factor was the cheapness of labour. It was cheaper than in the rest of Europe, excepting Russia[4] and parts of Italy. In addition to this, in the gold and silver trade there was a special rebate system in existence. In this the workers paid their foremen 20% of their wages for his having given them work; the foreman in his turn handed over this commission to the employer in order to protect his job. This in effect meant that the producers were able to put in for a higher than actual cost. It is not known whether Ratzersdorfer put out work to such workshops, but as his stock was so diversified in scope and quality he might well have taken advantage of this system.

From this prolific centre two distinct groups emerge. The first, already described, is the more expensive type of Renaissance object – either in rock-crystal or glass – wheel-cut in intaglio to resemble the celebrated Milanese originals [5][6] or perhaps in agate or a hardstone substitute; one of the more common models to appear is that of Diana the Huntress standing on the lip of a tazza, accompanied by her two dogs. The most elaborate Viennese productions include figures of ostriches – a popular model,

Left
Viennese enamel table ornament with a
bacchic scene.
Late 19th century.
About 6 in. high.
                              Sotheby & Co.

⁷ Palmer, op. cit., p. 127.

being a pun on the name *Oesterreich* – and the occasional hardstone figures
of swans. The second group comprises such diverse objects as caskets and
miniature furniture, all enamelled in tones of brown and pink. Many of
these have a distinctive vermiculated ground. There is no doubt that there
were several workshops first specialising in enamelled appliqués, since the
same panels often appear as components on different objects.

Carlsbad during the last quarter of the 19th century was one of the most
fashionable spas in Europe; Baedeker records that 40,000 visitors were
there in 1900 and although there were many shops selling Bohemian
glass to the tourists there were a few specialising in enamelled wares and
others in hardstones 'cut and set in an endless variety of artistic forms'.[7]
This might well have proved a profitable outlet to the jeweller.

The productions of Vienna were already 'dated' by 1914, and the
devastating effects of the First World War saw an end to this long and
successful production of luxuriously-unfunctional objects. Only the very
best Viennese work approaches that of Paris; the quality of enamelling
was never brilliantly executed and the choice of design sometimes
unsuitable for the type of object.

Right
A vase by Ratzersdorfer of Vienna, the
Lobmeyr glass body wheel-cut by Peter
Eisert.
Vienna, 1878.
16⅜ in. high.
          *Osterreichisches Museum für
                 angewandte Kunst*

Revival of Limoges Enamel

Limoges, a town in provincial France, had been famous for its output of enamels during the Middle Ages and the Renaissance. In the 13th century it had produced an endless stream of liturgical objects including *chasses*, *croziers* and book-covers, enamelled in the *champlevé* technique against a copper ground.

At the beginning of the 16th century it was again thriving, and this time it held a virtual monopoly of painted enamels. These were mostly in the form of oblong plaques painted *en grisaille* with mythological and religious scenes. Alternatively the same type of decoration was applied to vessels such as tazzas, salts and ewers. However, during the 17th century there was a decline in interest in painted enamels of this type and demand slackened. Yet from the late 15th century the town had been dominated by several family workshops, of which the longest to survive was that of the Nouailler family; the last member to continue the tradition was Jean-Baptiste II who died in 1804.[1]

It was ironical that this family should survive two centuries during which time their work was not in great demand, only to relinquish the art of enamelling just before there was to be a great revival of interest in Renaissance objects, and within a few years the demand had outstripped the available supplies.

In the first half of the 19th century there are several mentions of enamellers copying 'old Limoges': one of the best known was Julien Robillard of Paris. Yet it was not until the middle of the century that the real stimulus to revive a dead art was to come from the Sèvres porcelain factory. The director was a Monsieur Meyer-Heim who, together with a group of enamellers, encouraged by a subsidy from the State, investigated the technicalities of painted enamels and especially the Limousin process of the 16th century. They in turn trained others in the art of enamelling at Sèvres and by the mid-1860s there were several workshops in Paris producing Limoges enamels. Some of these were definitely made to deceive, since the value of genuine early pieces was rising all the time.

[1] Bourdery, L., *Les Émaux Peintes*, printed by V. H. Ducourtieux, Limoges, 1888, p. 207.

A tazza in Limoges style, signed *Auguste Wahrmund*.
1888.

Osterreichisches Museum für angewabdte Kunst

[2] ibid., pp. 217–23.

The peak of the Limoges revival came in the late 1880s when three major exhibitions were held in France and Germany. The most important was the retrospective exhibition held at Limoges itself in 1866; only painted enamels were included and such was the level of interest taken in this subject that the catalogue recorded an analysis of *contre-émail* colours,[2] which is the colour of the layer of enamel on the reverse of the copper plate. Also included in the exhibition were contemporary copies made in France and England.

Only three years before the Limoges Exhibition the best of the French enamellers had exhibited in Germany. By all accounts Nuremberg was very impressed by the works of Paul Soyer in 1883 but by the time of the Munich Exhibition in 1888 it was quite clear that Vienna was not lagging behind Sèvres in advancing the 'old techniques' of Limoges. The chemistry laboratory in the Museum in Vienna had been the main force behind this. Although the technique of Limoges enamels was being investigated it was only one of many that were undergoing scrutiny at a time when a serious attempt was being made to understand all old methods so as to restore

national treasures. Professor Hans Macht was the leading exponent at
that time and both his work and that of his pupils, notably Auguste
Wahrmund and Maria Stemkovska received high praise at Munich. A
casket executed by the latter in 1892 shows the transition from the restrained
Limousin *grisaille* style and the polychrome enamels more popular at the
turn of the century. Although her design is taken straight from a 16th
century engraving it displays a certain sense of space and composition
which was sadly lacking in the Parisian Limoges-style productions at that
time, in which the *grisaille* was 'improved' by the addition of a little chocolate brown which, according to Cunyngham, 'gave to the work the tone
of a photograph'.[3] He goes on to say that 'nothing can be more unpleasant
than this detestable pigment. Those who use it must surely be deficient
in a sense of colour.' After the middle of the 1890s the school of enamellers
produced little of unusual interest until the first examples of the modern
style came from the Wiener Werkstätte at the beginning of this century.
Meanwhile the firm of Ratzersdorfer and other retailers were having a
greater success with decorative objects made of alloy and painted with 17th
and 18th century frivolities.

    Meanwhile, in England, Limoges enamel both old and new was in vogue
with collectors, but there was no school propagating its manufacture. The
Arts and Crafts Movement had taken a grip and a rather crushing indict-
ment of Limoges is given by one of the movement's greatest enamellers,
who wrote in 1906 – 'The Limoges enamel is not a true expression of enamel.
The great majority of these old enamels have no *raison d'être* . . . for they
could have been done equally well in other materials not nearly so difficult
to achieve.'[4]

[3] Cunynghame, H., *European Enamels*, Me-
thuen & Co., London, 1906, p. 171.

[4] Fisher, A., *The Art of Enamelling on Metal*,
The Studio, London, 1906.

Russia in the 19th Century

Left
Russian double-opening cigarette case, decorated in *cloisonné* enamel and with a bear-hunting scene.
$4\frac{1}{2}$ in. wide.

Sotheby & Co.

Russia, in the production of objects of vertu in the 19th century, stood apart from the rest of Europe. There had been a very strong French and German influence on the design and creation of works of art in the previous century, but the mediæval revival which occurred in Europe during the second quarter of the century compelled artists and craftsmen to look back to the more glorious days of the 17th century for inspiration; it was then that more current techniques of enamelling had reached Russia through Holland and Greece.

It was at the Great Exhibition that Western Europeans were able to examine a comprehensive selection of objects from Moscow and St Petersburg. What impressed many of the visitors and reviewers was the series of monumental urns and architectural devices such as door surrounds entirely veneered in malachite. This was the speciality of the firm of Demidoff of St Petersburg who seemed to have a virtual monopoly on this particular stone since they owned the most productive mines in the Urals. But even more impressive to most observers were the silver-gilt figures of peasants made and shown by the firm of Ignace Sasikoff, the Imperial goldsmith, who later had offices in St Petersburg as well as Moscow.

Right
The Coronation Egg. Presented to Alexandra Feodorovna by Nicholas II in 1897. The 'surprise' contained inside is a scale model of the Imperial Coach used the previous year at their coronation in Moscow. 5 in. high.

Wartski, London

Nearly all the pieces that they showed at the Great Exhibition were northern
in feeling; there was very little hint of outside influences in the vodka sets,
drinking-horns and historical figures which they had on their stand.
Even by the time of the 1867 Exhibition the only type of object which
displayed external influence was a series of ivory tankards with silver
mounts, copies and versions of the 17th century German type that were
being sought after by collectors. There were many such art collectors
amongst the nobility of Russia at this time and their taste in collecting
is reflected in these objects.

During the previous century nearly all the more splendid *kovsch* were
made of silver and then decorated in *niello* (oxydised silver). The popularity
of *niello* really never abated until fairly late in the 19th century. Yet after
1870 in addition to the firm of Sasikoff, the firms of Paul Outchinnikoff
of Moscow and John Khlebnikof dominate the Russian scene with their
productions ranging from cigarette cases to vodka sets and *kovschi* in silver
enamelled in the old Russian style mostly in the *cloisonné* technique. Their
interpretations were not particularly varied, and their designs thought to
be a little heavy, so much so that in 1892 Ferdinand Luthmer,[1] Professor
and Director of the Kunstgewerbeschule and Kunstgewerbemuseum in
Frankfurt commenting on the three leading firms said that 'their wares do
not appeal to European eyes due to their harsh colours'. Europe for the most
part held this opinion for the next eight years, until the works of Peter
Carl Fabergé were first exhibited internationally at Paris in 1900. This was
the first time that his series of Easter eggs made for the Imperial family
were seen outside Russia; these, together with other pieces from his stock,
earned him the highest possible praise. Above all, Paris recognised his
craftsmanship, which in quality was hardly equalled in the rest of Europe.

[1] Luthmer, op. cit., pp. 200–1.

[2] Snowman, A. K., *The Art of Carl Fabergé* (in Bibliography).

Fabergé

The Fabergés had left France shortly after the Revocation of the Edict of Nantes in 1685, which denied religious freedom to the Huguenots,[2] and by 1842 they were established in St Petersburg. Gustav Fabergé, Carl's father, worked with the well-known firm of Keibel before taking the step of setting himself up as a goldsmith and jeweller in his own right in St Petersburg. At the beginning it was a modest firm which concentrated on jewellery and so it remained throughout Carl Fabergé's childhood. Gustav

Red-gold strut clock, enamelled in translucent pale green against an engraved *moirée* ground.
Workmaster, Henrik Wigström.
6⅞ in. high.

Private collection

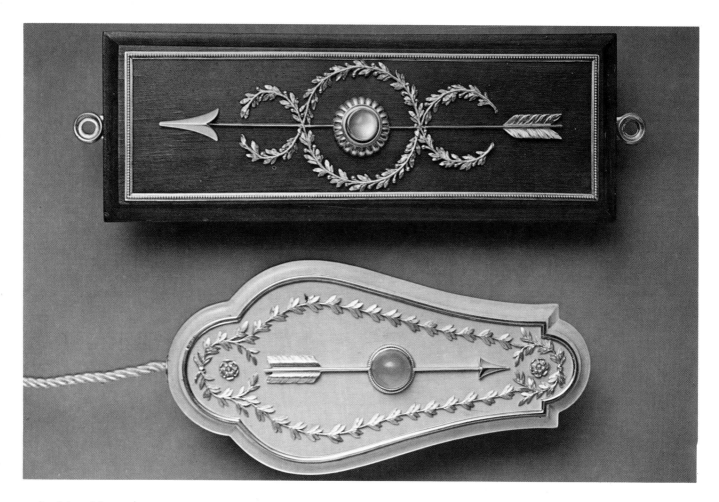

Two bell pushes with palisander and hollywood bases, silver mounts in Louis XVI style.
Fabergé workmaster A.
$7\frac{1}{4}$ in. and 6 in. long.

Wartski, London

retired in 1860 and went to live in Dresden, and for ten years the firm was put under the control of a manager. When Gustav's eldest son Carl had finished his studies in St Petersburg he was put through a period of apprenticeship away from St Petersburg and sent travelling around Europe to learn English, French and Italian. Starting in Dresden he progressed from there to Frankfurt-am-Main where he was apprenticed to Herr Friedmann, one of the best-known goldsmiths in Germany at that period. This was followed by a few months in Florence and London, ending up in Paris. There is no doubt that during this time he was much impressed by the different types of goldsmiths work that he had seen in the various cities, which must have contrasted severely with the pieces which he knew from his mother country. The 'old Russian' style was still prevalent in Russia; however, Fabergé, having seen what was going on during this, the most eclectic period of the 19th century, returned to work under the manager of his father's shop in St Petersburg until 1870. It was then that he was given the job of running the entire enterprise at the age of twenty-four. It turned out to be an auspicious year; the 'English Shop', which had been run by two Englishmen, and had been the most fashionable and well-patronised jewellery and silver shop in St Petersburg closed down and it was lucky for Carl Fabergé that the Court transferred their patronage to his shop.

Yet it was not until 1884 that the real break-through came for the House of Fabergé in St Petersburg. It was in that year that Alexander III had presented an elaborate jewelled Easter egg to his wife, Maria. This was the first of fifty-six celebrated Imperial Easter eggs which were created for the two last Russian Tsars, Alexander III and Nicholas II.

After Alexander's death, Nicholas continued the custom of ordering two eggs each year, one for his wife and one for his mother. The choice of materials and the design were left entirely to Fabergé, who surrounded the construction of the annual order of eggs with a cloak of absolute secrecy, reminiscent of the weeks preceding an important fashion show today.

[3] Massie, R. K., *Nicholas and Alexandra*, Atheneum, New York, 1967, pp. 166–7.

The Easter celebrations, which included the giving of presents, and had really helped build up the name of Fabergé in the outside world, were taken more seriously in Russia than in any other European country. It was the climax of the Orthodox Church year and 'more profoundly holy and more joyous than Christmas'. On Easter Night, after the service, the Russian Easter festivities began.[3] Because eggs, butter and cheese had been denied them during Lent, the climax of the feasts was *paskha*, a rich creamy dessert, and *kulitch*, the round Easter cake. In the Crimea, where the Imperial family celebrated the occasion, because it was a tradition that any stranger was welcome and must be entertained, the Imperial Palace became a vast banquetting hall. Presiding over this Nicholas and Alexandra greeted the entire household with the traditional three kisses of blessing, welcome and joy. To the members of the court and the Imperial Guard the sovereigns gave their famous Easter eggs. Some were simple – well-painted egg-shells from which the contents had been blown. Alternatively, they gave enamelled porcelain eggs suspended on silk ribbons, or to the very fortunate, miniature eggs made of gold and silver and enamelled in translucent colours by Fabergé. These could be attached to chains to eventually form necklaces or bracelets.

It was the success of the first Imperial egg in 1884 which prompted the Tzar to grant Fabergé the Royal Warrant. The success of his Easter eggs of all types had proved to Fabergé that his Russian and foreign clients admired his inventiveness and would probably provide a market for expensive trinkets.

The vast majority of jewellers in Europe at that time had completely given in to the demands of the fashionable for gem-set brooches and other jewels. The criteria of a good jewel was whether or not the stones were large enough or expensive enough. Little thought was given to elegance of design and by producing jewels and personal accessories such as cuff-links, studs, cigarette cases and pencil holders which displayed strength of design and execution he broadened the type of object he could offer to his customers. His visit to the Grünes Gewölbe in Dresden, when only an apprentice, had obviously left a lasting impression in his mind. Here he had seen all the rich and expensive objects made for the Electors of Saxony, including the series of miniature Pageants made by Dinglinger. His expansion really started in 1884. To a large extent his commercial success must have depended on the 'workmaster' system which he had evolved. Not all his workmen, who numbered nearly five-hundred at the beginning of the century, were officially employed by him. Many of them owed their allegiance to the owners of small specialist firms whose total output was commissioned and bought by Fabergé. The owners were called 'workmasters' and it is their marks which are to be found more often than not beside the signature of the House and the Russian gold and silver marks. So Fabergé's position at the height of his success could be described as an 'impresario-retailer', a position which must have been comparable to that of Rudolfi of Paris in the middle of the century and his contemporary Ratzersdorfer in Vienna.

As Court Jeweller to the Tzar of Russia, his clients were international. King Edward VII was a regular customer and was always pleading with Fabergé that 'We must have no duplicates'. Until the Exposition Internationale Universelle in Paris in 1900 Fabergé was really only known by those Royal Families of Europe who could be numbered as his customers and by several rich families in Russia.

It was at the Exhibition that the complete set of Easter eggs was shown and together with his other pieces earned him a gold medal and a Légion d'Honneur from the French Government. This, the highest award given internationally, must have assured his continued success. From 1900 until the outbreak of war fourteen years later, his workshops never let-up the production of every conceivable type of object. When war came it was quite obviously a threat to the purveyor of the most luxurious of luxury commodities satisfying the demand of European Royalty and the very rich. Business wound down; some of his clients were no longer able to indulge in his things since they were on the other side, whilst others felt twinges of social conscience and ordered objects of base metal. Still the endless line of eggs continued, although as the war got worse so the magnificence was stripped away and a utilitarian look sustituted (see plate   p. 106). Part of Fabergé's workshop was given over to the war effort and by the time of the final blow, the Revolution, his art was doomed. Fabergé himself managed to escape to Switzerland, disguised as a diplomat, where he died two years later.

Fabergé's work is perhaps too recent to put it in perspective. He was undoubtedly one of the most prolific of any period and as so many of his works survive today it is possible to attempt an assessment of the lasting qualities of his work. As a craftsman and designer he must be placed alongside other 19th century artists who have revived previous styles. By the time the House of Fabergé was really under way the mediaeval and Renaissance revival was past. His inspiration was derived mainly from 18th century originals. It is only in a very few fields that he emerges as an original designer – yet in everything he made his standard of craftsmanship can be compared favourably with that of the original. In the middle of the 19th century a goldsmith exhibitor was complaining that no box-maker could make a hinge which operated successfully after a few months.[4] Yet here was a craftsman who insisted that his workmen should attain a level of excellence in box making which had not been reached since the days of Vachette. The sureness of quality is to be found in all his objects of vertu which were derived and adapted from 18th century originals. Strangely enough one finds a greater degree of 'lightness' in his own original works – such as new-fangled bell pushes (see plate 118, p. 108) – than in his versions of 18th century snuff-boxes. In the former his metalwork is combined with hardstone or enamel and the effect is pleasing, whereas in the field of snuff-boxes Fabergé's workmen were inhibited by the designs of the 18th century which they could only produce in a thicker gauge of metal, thus producing a 'heavy' effect. Yet it is the same heaviness which prevails in Henri Dassons' copies of 18th century furniture. In all 19th century revivalists' work there is an inherent ponderous quality which cannot be obliterated.

Fabergé's productions can be divided into two types – the unfunctional and the functional. In the former the series of Easter eggs made for the Imperial family stand out as the most extravagant examples which were to elevate the name and international fame of the House of Fabergé above all his competitors. After the eggs he is perhaps best known for his hardstone figures of animals and for the small group of miniature figures taken from Russian life. He cannot really be called the introducer into society of either of these, yet his interpretation transformed the originals. There is no doubt that he must have been inspired and influenced to produce animals by having seen the works of the French Animalier School of animal sculptors. As a jeweller and craftsman he obviously saw the potential sale for finely carved hardstone miniatures which would probably appeal to feminine taste more than would those of bronze. He was himself a collector of *netsuke*, Japanese carved ivory and wood toggles, and these made him aware of the tactile qualities of small animal carvings and at the same time probably helped him determine the scale of his productions, so that they average twice the size of *netsuke*. His animals were an instant success and continued to remain so, partly because he used numerous different hardstones – not only those quarried from the mines in the Urals but others bought from foreign dealers.

Animals both domestic and wild were modelled in miniature. The craftsmen made great use of the natural colours and striations of any particular stone. But if it was necessary to alter the surface colour, it could be done in agate with stain. Alternatively the same stone can be turned into black onyx by boiling it in honey and then carbonising the sugar content with a soak in sulphuric acid. However, there was one colour that could not be found in a natural specimen. This was sealing-wax red. This deficiency was made good for Fabergé by a craftsman at the Imperial

[4]See 'Illustrated Catalogue of the Paris 1867 Exhibition', *Art Journal*, Virtue & Co, London and New York, 1868, p. 274.

A group of hardstone animals with jewelled
eyes by Fabergé, of various stones including
white chalcedony, agate, aventurine quartz,
grey kalgan jasper, nephrite, rhodonite,
amazonite and topaz quartz.
Siberian jade elephant: 2½ in. long.
Private collection

Glass Factory, called Petouchov, who developed a strong glass substitute
which is known as purpurine.

Other extravagances in hardstone which could be bought from the shops
in Moscow and St Petersburg included a large selection of flowers set in
vases, for which rock-crystal was inevitably used. This gave the illusion
that it was a glass vase filled with water; the crystal was bored to accommodate the silver or gold stem which ran from the edge of the bottom
and rested on the top rim. In post-Revolution copies the stem can sometimes be found standing up almost perpendicular as if supported by the
water alone.

The most functional of Fabergé's range of accessories were his cigarette
cases. These are in all qualities and of three main types. Firstly, the double-
opening case, in which both sides contained a row of cigarettes; the
second was closer to a snuff-box, with a lid not fitted for cigarettes; and the
third had a sprung lid which was activated by pressing a jewelled thumb-
piece. These were the three most usual types, but of course it was possible
to commission any shape which struck one's fancy. Leopold de Rothschild
didn't commission particularly unusually designed objects, but instead
gave his friends conventional Fabergé pieces such as sealing-wax cases,
vesta cases for matches or pencils beautifully enamelled in his own racing
colours of royal blue and yellow in stripes, a particularly pleasing
combination.

It is perhaps on cigarette cases that Fabergé produced some of his best
combinations of materials. Some are enamelled *en plein* in one colour, that is
with the whole outer surface covered in enamel, except for the mounts;
whilst others are decorated with a combination of colours. Customers had

144 colours to choose from, and if they should prefer to have gold boxes instead the choices varied between plain engine-turned cases or a very expensive combination of different coloured stripes of gold. Invariably the thumb-pieces are set with diamond chips. Should neither of the standard types of box attract the customer there was another very distinctive type which was available. This was the box constructed in the *samorodok* technique (see plate 119, p. 113). Resembling craters on the moon, with a rough surface, this was achieved by bringing the metal plate almost up to melting point and then quickly removing it from the fire: the sudden reduction in temperature shrank the plate which gave it this rough nugget-like surface.

Amongst the less functional 'objects of function' which he made are the miniature frames, used either for photographs or painted miniatures, which are elaborate versions of the large range of mid-19th century Daguerreotype frames made by the wood-workers of Austria and which were reductions of Louis XV and Louis XVI picture frames.[5] Fabergé substituted gold or silver and enamel for wood and perhaps the reason why there was a revival in the art of portrait miniature painting was

[5] ibid., p. 262.

A Fabergé hardstone and enamelled gold figure of a *pirozhnik*, the pie-seller with Algerian onyx smock, partly covered with an opaque white chalcedony apron, lapis lazuli hat and gem-set eyes.
Workmaster, Henrik Wigström.
$4\frac{3}{4}$ in. high.

Sotheby & Co.

A Fabergé two-colour-gold double-opening
cigarette case.
Workmaster, August Hollming.
$3\frac{3}{4}$ in. wide.

Sotheby & Co.

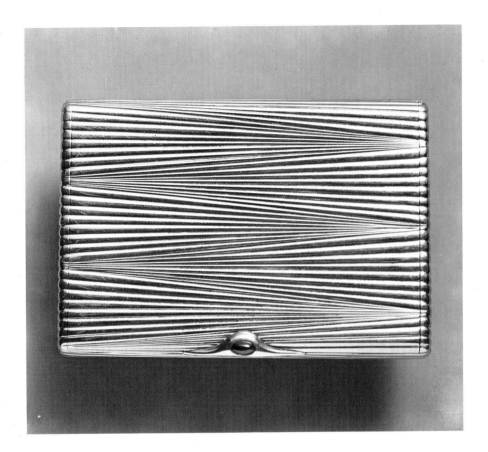

A Fabergé silver cigarette case, decorated
in the *samarodok* finish.
Workmaster, Wilhelm August Hollming.
4 in. long.

Wartski, London

because photographs, as yet not in colour, looked drab inside such a splendidly rich surround. Yet the name Fabergé did not evoke an image of practical simplicity; his stock was enlarged year by year to include yet more and more objects – in their simple unembellished form, mostly functional, but as enriched by Fabergé, considerably less so. He produced every conceivable type of accessory, to a greater extent even than goldsmiths in the 18th century in France when richly-produced accessories to life were *de rigueur*.

A gold and enamelled dog whistle, a gold-mounted and jewelled thermometer and a white onyx stamp dampener seem very much out of context in that period of the late 19th century when industrialisation and standardisation of the everyday things in life was well under way. Fabergé had really resurrected the whole field of objects of vertu during the two decades before the outbreak of war. His business was run as if it was in existence under the patronage of the Crown before the French Revolution. He had been an impresario in a revivalist age and it is very sad that his craftsmanship and invention could not have been used during the 1920s, a period which artistically is identified by its geometric line.

A group of objects of vertu by Fabergé, including a pair of Bezique markers, a vodka cup in rock crystal, the gold mounts in art nouveau taste, and a cane handle. Bezique markers, 4¼ in. wide.

Wartski, London

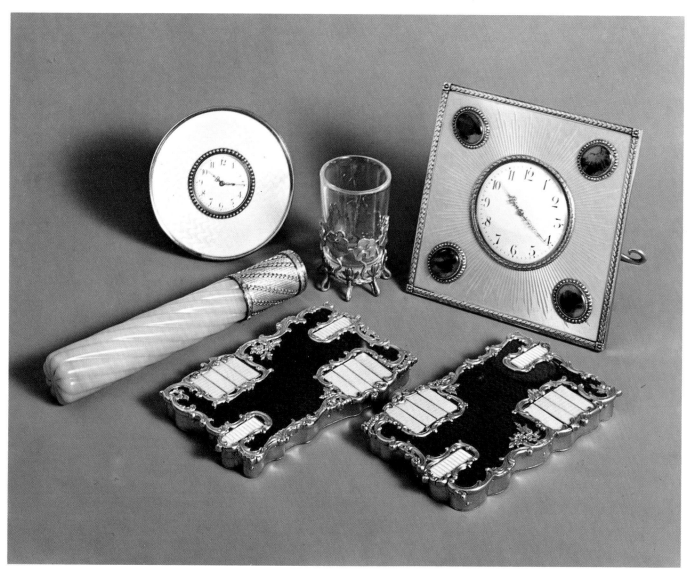

Arts and Crafts
and Art Nouveau

A dish by Fernand Thesmar, enamelled *pliqué à jour*.
$3\frac{1}{2}$ in. diameter.
Victoria and Albert Museum

PLAT PORTE-CARTE, Cloisonné sur bronze, dia-
mètre, 0^m30. Prix:. . . **24 50.**
Sur socle en bois de fer. . **32** fr.

An advertisement in *La Vie Parisienne* showing an imported Chinese *cloisonné* enamel,
complete with stand, for 56 francs 50.
1880.

Cased glass scent bottle, with gold mounts of Moghul inspiration, by Tiffany and Co. of New York.
2¼ in. high.

Sotheby & Co.

[1] Fisher, op. cit., plate 18.

[2] *La Vie Parisienne*, 18 September, 1880, p. 541.

[3] Cunynghame, op. cit., p. 171

Left
An enamelled plaque set within a silver frame, by Alexander Fisher.
16 in. long.

Sotheby & Co.

'Enamels should never be copies of anything in nature, nor of any other process of painting in art. They should be creations.'

Alexander Fisher (1907)

It was at the 1862 Exhibition in London that the origins of two movements which were to influence the course of art in the latter part of the century in Europe were first seen. The first was the display of imported Japanese works of art; the second was the exhibition of furniture made by Morris & Co. The first was the greatest influence on decoration in the late 19th century and was that in which linear economy was propagated. In the second, the importance of Morris's stand lay in the fact that this was the first time that the public were shown his ideas, which over the next fifteen years were to evolve into the foundation of the Arts and Crafts Movement.

It wasn't until three years later that William Morris, together with Ruskin, preached the new doctrine to overthrow the whole industrial system itself. They were preaching against Elkington and every other manifestation of industry in art. Morris and Ruskin recognised the dangers of a commercially-based policy on applied arts and in their analysis Morris stated that the 'rich must learn to love art more than riches' and that the poor should 'hate joyless labour more than poverty'.

Without Morris the Century Guild would never have been founded in 1881 and the Art Workers Guild in 1884. Four years later the Guild of Handicrafts was formed. So by the 1890s the Arts and Crafts Movement was well under way, Morris had closed the wide gap which had previously existed between fine and applied arts, and he was encouraging his disciples to search for a style that could institute a sense of design. Many artists gave up careers in order to devote their time to designing, so much so that Walter Crane, who had founded the Art Workers Guild, pointed out that it was 'turning our artists into craftsmen and our craftsmen into artists'.

During the 1890s this return to hand-made objects brought about the decline in manufactured pieces, but it did produce a revival in the art of enamelling in England, with one or two notable names. The main voice of the movement was *Studio*, a periodical which recorded all the most important changes.

Japanese and Chinese influences on the production of enamelled objects between 1862 and 1890 can best be seen in the manufactured works by Barbedienne and Elkington; however, these imported objects,[1] nearly all in *cloisonné* technique, inspired an enameller of the former factory, named Fernand Thesmar, to take up this type of work.[2] He generally signed his work with a monogram, and although most of his works were of *cloisonné* enamel he sometimes worked in *plique-à-jour* technique. This transparent form of enamelling was to prove very popular in France with the jewellers; it was also popular in Russia and in the Baltic countries. Resembling stained glass, it is particularly attractive when used for bowls or cups, which when placed under a light look like a honeycomb of metal filled with enamel 'windows'. The secret in the production of *plique-à-jour* enamels was that for the duration of the firing a metal base is used as a support, but when the piece has cooled and hardened the 'base' is removed. A *plique-à-jour* enamelled bowl by Thesmar with an art nouveau design of carnations is dated 1893. His work is close to Chinese export wares with a strong hint of European art nouveau design creeping in. His work in *cloisonné* is rather repetitive and is as solid as Barbedienne's productions.

Meanwhile, in England, enamelling had fallen into disuse after the closures of the Staffordshire factories earlier in the century. Ruskin so bewailed this fact that he offered a prize for the best piece of enamelling in *champlevé* style in 1860.[3] It was won by a jeweller who seemed only to have produced this one piece and then discontinued his productions. It wasn't until 1885 that a French enameller called Dalpayrat came to the South Kensington Museum, where, as in other museums, notably in Vienna and Germany, investigations were being made into the art of enamelling. He gave a series of lectures and two of these were attended by Alexander

Fisher, the son of a Staffordshire potter, who was to emerge as England's greatest enameller at the turn of this century. He was most interested in the different effects that could be achieved in enamelling. He had only two lessons and worked out the rest for himself. In his book Fisher said 'Let us then start by thinking of enamels as creations, not copies, made as it were, of precious stones, only with this difference – that instead of a narrow range, they are capable of an infinite variety of colouration . . . they should be creations'. His works are just that.

Commercial objects of vertu in art nouveau style were being produced by the firm of Liberty in London. Nearly all their productions were in silver and they employed a group of designers to make their jewellery, cigarette boxes and other trinkets for them. They never disclosed the names of their designers; they were aided in this by the Assay Laws which allowed retailers to have their own mark. This could not happen in France where the actual craftsman was obliged to mark his own pieces. Even after sixty years it is not absolutely clear who did what; yet one piece was definitely designed by Archibald Knox.

Three enamel boxes by Professor O. Prutscher, A. Berger and A. von Stark. The latter is in *cloisonné* technique. Vienna: 1908, 1914 and 1911 $4\frac{1}{2}$ $5\frac{1}{2}$ in. wide.

Osterreichisches Museum für angewandte Kunst

Art nouveau was one of the last great craft movements in which the skill of execution matched and enhanced artistic invention. In France at the turn of the century the most notable goldsmiths' work was in the field of jewellery design. For those who preferred art nouveau jewellery to brooches and necklaces set with expensive stones there were several great jewellers from whom one could either commission a piece or choose one from stock. René Lalique and Henri Vever in collaboration with Eugène Grasset in Paris, Philipe Wolfers in Brussels and Luis Masriera in Barcelona

A Fabergé table lamp with Loetz Witwe glass body made for the Tzar's yacht. Workmaster: Johann Victor Aarne. (excluding shade). 11 in. high.
Wartski, London

are the most important of this school. Lalique, however, stands above the rest due to his experiments in different materials, such as horn and ivory, and for his designs which tended to be either floral or incorporating a sinuous female. To these designers precious stones were for the *parvenu*. Artistry counted most of all. They were particularly fond of *plique-à-jour* enamelling. Since this book is not really concerned with jewellery we can only acknowledge the fact that the most inventive goldsmiths' work since the 18th century is to be found in their works.[4] Louis Comfort Tiffany in New York also designed jewels and small objects (see pl. 123 p. 117). His long-established family firm had produced silverware and decorative objects of a conventional type. He was first exposed to foreign influences at the Philadelphia Centennial Exhibition of 1876 and after that he travelled in Europe and started experimenting in glass.[5] He was fascinated most by opalescent glass and it is this buried, antique-like look which is the hallmark of his work. Yet as shown here in the gold mounted scent bottle, the glass body is worked in a way similar to Galle's style and is inspired by Chinese snuff bottles.

It is really the work of these two men, followed by that of the firm of Loetz Witwe in Bohemia, that revolutionised the whole manufacture of glass. Their products, unconventional, decorative, and in a commercialised form not expensive for the collector, together with jewellery, are the two most successful manifestations of an eclectic style which, because it was misinterpreted by so many artist craftsmen, has until recently been derided. Yet it must be recognised as the hotbed from which the modern movement emerged. Hints of a sterner geometric line appear in the boxes made in Vienna between 1908 and 1911. Art nouveau had arrived in Vienna somewhat belatedly. The Secessionist Movement was founded in 1897 to unite the avant-garde artists into a central organisation. It was to become an international centre of new directions in art and design.

The First World War saw the end of art nouveau, Fabergé and a revivalist age. It was a machine-age war run on conventional lines which proved disastrous for all participants. Social life, such as it had existed at the turn of the century, could not continue on the same plane. A more utilitarian mode of life was imposed on those who before the war had been the patrons of craftsmen. The making of objects of vertu suffered; yet the objects themselves were now more or less obsolete. As smoking became more popular, so manufacturers improved cigarette cartons to make them strong enough to eliminate the bother of transferring the cigarettes into a silver or gold case. Electricity at the turn of the century had brought in the electric fan ventilator which forced the fan into exile; in any case a fan would have been most incongruous with the short 1920s skirts and new dashing style. Better ventilation and drainage relegated the vinaigrette to a drawer and whilst the Swiss continued to enamel their watches in a 1920s taste the majority of other useful accessories were left undecorated, and the scent producers of the period made their own bottles.

Above all, the motor car now emerged as the status symbol which was not only functional but could, if necessary, be very expensive as well as look very expensive. So the maker of objects of vertu was now almost completely redundant; the motor-manufacturer could supply a functional machine decorated to the whims of the new owner who, if sufficiently egocentric, realised that his new toy would, on a long journey, be admired by a larger audience than would see his cigarette case. And if that wasn't enough, there was always an air trophy to go after!

[4] For further details see *Studio*, 1901, p. 25.

[5] Museum of Modern Art, *Art Nouveau*, edited by Peter Selz and Mildred Constantine, distributed by Doubleday, New York, 1959.

Select Bibliography
and Index

Select Bibliography

GENERAL

Boehn, Max von, *Modes and Manners*, 4 vols, Harrap & Co, London, 1935.
D'Allemagne, Henry René, *Les Accessoires du Costume et du Mobilier*, Schemit, Paris, 1928.
Evans, Dr Joan, *Pattern – A Study of Ornament in Western Europe (1180–1900)*, Oxford University Press, 1931.

SNUFFBOXES

Bramsen, Bo, *Nordiske Snusdäser*, Politikens Vorlag, Copenhagen, 1965.
Berry-Hill, Henry and Sidney, *Antique Gold Boxes*, Abelard Press, New York, 1960.
Corbeille, Clare le, *European and American Snuffboxes*, Batsford, London, 1966.
Duvaux, Lazare, *Livre-Journal*, 2 vols, Paris, 1873.
Nocq, Henry, *Tabatières, boîtes et etuis, Orfèvreries de Paris Musée du Louvre*, Les Éditions G. van Oest, Paris, 1925.
Norton, Richard and Martin, *A History of Gold Snuff-boxes*, S. J. Phillips Ltd, London, 1938.
Snowman, A. Kenneth, *Eighteenth Century Gold Boxes of Europe*, Faber & Faber, London, 1966.

HORN AND TORTOISE-SHELL

Dent, H. C., *Piqué – a beautiful Minor Art*, Connoisseur, London, 1923.
Phillips, P. A. S., *John Obrisset*, Batsford, London, 1931.

SWISS AUTOMATA

Chapuis, A., *Histoire de la boîte à musique*, Éditions du Journal d'Horlogerie et de Bijouterie, Lausanne, 1955.
Chapuis, A., and Droz, E., *Les Automates*, Editions du Griffan, Neuchatel, n.d.
Chapuis, A., and Gélis, E., *Le Monde des Automates*, Paris, 1928.

ENGLISH PAINTED ENAMELS

Pazaurek, G. E., *Deutsche Fayence und Porzellan Hausmaler*, 2 vols, privately printed, Leipzig, 1925.
Rackham, B., *Catalogue of the Schreiber Collection*, Victoria and Albert Museum, Department of Ceramics, vol. III, 'Enamels and Glass', published under the authority of the Board of Education, 1924.
Mew, E., *Battersea Enamels*, Medici Society, London, 1926.
Hughes, T. and B., *English Painted Enamels*, Country Life, London, 1951.
Watney, B., and Charleston, R., *Transactions of the English Ceramic Circle*, vol. VI, part II, London, 1966.
Watney, B., 'English enamels in the 18th century', *Antiques International*, Michael Joseph, London, 1966.

RUSSIAN ENAMELS AND OBJECTS OF VERTU

Bainbridge, H. C., *Peter Carl Fabergé, His Life and Work*, Batsford, London, 1949.
Ross, M. C., *The Art of Karl Fabergé and His Contemporaries*. University of Oklahoma Press, 1965.
Snowman, A. Kenneth, *The Art of Carl Fabergé*, Faber & Faber, London, 1962 (2nd edition).

Index